Shocking Science

Fun & Fascinating Electrical Experiments

Shar Levine & Leslie Johnstone

illustrated by Emily S. Edliq

Sterling Publishing Co., Inc.
New York

To Paul, a wonderful husband, an incredible father, and my best friend. A former electronic engineer, with a penchant for blowing things up, Paul spent countless hours helping with the activities in this book. It is to his credit that he eventually saw the light, and is now a brilliant and successful lawyer. Thanks, dear. And to Shira — you're now a high school grad! — S. L.

To Melissa, Lawrence, Joe, Ian, and Jessica Davidson. — L. J.

To all my dear friends, especially Lesley and Raynell. Thanks for always being there to share life's experiences, no matter how busy we all get. You are true friends. — E. E.

To my darling daughter, Rachel, who makes it all worthwhile. — J. C.

Acknowledgments

The authors would like to thank the following for their assistance: Anchor Appliances; BC Hydro; Lens and Shutter; R. P. Electronics; Debbie Roman from Ballard Power Systems; Eugene and Sharon Cisneros of the Mineralogical Research Company; Teresa Wilson; Karen Thomas; Brian Yu; Dr. Peter Cooperberg of St. Paul's Hospital, Vancouver; Jim Weise of Science World; Otha H. ("Skeet") Vaughan of NASA; the amazing Emily Edliq; and Jeff Connery of Printed Light. Thanks also to Brendan O'Grady, Matthew Hallaran, and the Science 10 Enriched class for the great electric motor designs. Last but not least, thanks to Holly and Dr. Roger Sharf for the information on EKGs.

Designed by Judy Morgan. Edited by Isabel Stein.

Library of Congress Cataloging-in-Publication Data

Levine, Shar, 1953-
    Shocking Science: fun & fascinating electrical experiments / Shar Levine & Leslie
Johnstone; illustrated by Emily S. Edliq.
        p. cm.
    Includes index.
    Summary: Suggest experiments studying static electricity and electrical circuits, with easily obtained supplies. Includes historical information and glossary.
    ISBN 0-8069-3946-X
    1. Electricity—Experiments—Juvenile literature. [1. Electricity—Experiments. 2. Experiments.] I. Johnstone, Leslie. II. Title.

QC527.2 .L48 1999
537'.078—dc21

99-043501

3 5 7 9 10 8 6 4 2

First paperback edition published in 2000 by
Sterling Publishing Company, Inc.
387 Park Avenue South, New York, N.Y. 10016
© 1999 by Shar Levine & Leslie Johnstone
Distributed in Canada by Sterling Publishing
% Canadian Manda Group, One Atlantic Avenue, Suite 105
Toronto, Ontario, Canada M6K 3E7
Distributed in Great Britain and Europe by Chris Lloyd
463 Ashley Road, Parkstone, Poole, Dorset, BH14 0AX, England
Distributed in Australia by Capricorn Link (Australia) Pty Ltd.
P.O. Box 6651, Baulkham Hills, Business Centre, NSW 2153, Australia

Sterling ISBN 0-8069-3946-X Trade
0-8069-2271-0 Paper

Contents

Introduction

Have you ever thought about how electricity affects your life? Next time there is a power outage, you'll realize just how much you depend on it! It would be difficult to live without electricity. It allows us to turn on our lights. It powers our appliances. And where would computers be without electrical power?

Defining electricity is a difficult thing to do because there is no obvious answer. The first thing that comes to mind when you hear the word "electricity" is probably that it's the stuff which turns on your lights or operates anything that is plugged into the wall sockets. That's correct, but it is much more than that. Electricity is many things. In this book you will learn about the different ways electricity can be described.

You will travel in the footsteps of the early pioneers of electricity. You can try some experiments with static electricity that may make objects seem to move by themselves, or even cause hair-raising experiences!

You will also learn the practical aspects of electricity by performing safe and easy experi-

ments. You will learn how to make a simple motor, create a generator, and even design your own circuit board.

You'll get to learn an international language of symbols for electrical components. We've made this book easy to use by planning the experiments with electrical circuits so you can use something called a breadboard. This is a plastic board with built-in connections, to which you can attach things. These boards are inexpensive and are available in most electronics stores. The advantage of using a breadboard is that there is no soldering needed to complete the circuits and it is relatively simple for even young children to manage.

Many of the activities in this book could be used as the basis for a science fair project. See if one of the experiments interests you enough to investigate further.

NOTE TO PARENTS AND TEACHERS

Electricity experiments are among the most exciting science activities you can do with children. Children can't believe that a light bulb, attached to a battery with bits of wire, lights up. The activities in this book are safe and child-tested, and are structured so that the first time a technique or concept is introduced, it is described in detail. In the projects that follow, there are references to the experiments where the techniques are first explained, so you can return to them if necessary. Scientific words are defined the first time they are used, and many also appear in the glossary at the back of the book.

Electricity experiments have evolved over the years. There was a time when you needed things called Fahnestock clips or solder and a soldering iron to create a circuit board. If you wish, you can still use the traditional method of soldering or creating your own board by clipping wires together, but this book is designed to let you create circuits without soldering, using a breadboard. Closely following the instructions will ensure success.

SAFETY FIRST

Before you begin any of the activities in the book, there are a few do's and don'ts you need to follow so that you can do them all safely.

DO'S

1. Ask an adult before handling any materials or equipment.

2. Have an adult handle all sharp objects, such as knives, wire cutters, or razor blades.

3. Wash your hands after performing the experiments.

4. Tie back long hair while you work, and avoid wearing clothing with long, loose sleeves, which could knock things over.

5. Read all the steps of any experiment carefully and be sure you know what to do before you begin.

6. Always work in a well-ventilated area with adequate light.

7. Keep your work area clean and well organized. Make sure you have all the things you need before you start. Follow the project instructions regarding electronic components, battery sizes and procedures.

8. Tell an adult immediately if you hurt yourself in any way.

9. Keep all supplies, tools, chemicals, and experiments out of the reach of very young children.

10. Dispose of batteries in a safe manner. Check with your local garbage service for disposal information. Do not throw them in a fire. Do not use if the battery is leaking or is damaged in any way. If you see a crust or fluid on the outside, do not use or touch the battery; chemicals may have leaked out.

11. Wear safety goggles when cutting and stripping wires.

12. Look up any unfamiliar terms in the glossary before starting.

DON'TS

1. Do not taste, eat, or drink any of the experiments.

2. Do not do any of the experiments in this book with the electricity coming from the wall socket.

3. Do not stick your tongue on a battery terminal.

4. Do not go outdoors during a lightning storm. Stay indoors and turn off your TV and computer.

5. Do not connect the terminals of any battery directly together with a wire, as the battery and wire will heat up and could be damaged.

6. Do not mix up old and new batteries or alkaline and standard batteries. This can cause damage to the batteries; they could heat up or even leak.

7. At some science museums and in some classrooms, there are specialized pieces of equipment that demonstrate principles of electricity. A Van de Graaff generator and a Tesla coil are specially constructed devices that cannot be safely made at home; don't even think about it. Visit a museum that features one of these and ask a staff person for a demonstration, instead.

LIST OF EQUIPMENT & SUPPLIES

You can purchase most of the supplies needed at an electronics store. If you need extra supplies, consult the yellow pages of your telephone directory under "electronics," or try specialty stores. Some experiments may require additional supplies, which for the most part can be found around the house. Read each experiment through before you begin. Before you get started, you need to have the following basic supplies and equipment handy. **Note:** an asterisk (*) below means the term is defined in the glossary.

ELECTRONIC SUPPLIES:

batteries:

- 3 AA batteries
- One 9-volt (9 V) battery
- One 6-volt lantern battery

battery holder for 2 AA batteries and snap connector for battery holder

motor: 3-volt direct current* (DC) electric motor

small disc-shaped magnet and bar magnet

buzzer (1.5 to 3 V)

compass

capacitor* 16 V, 47 μF

jump wires* purchased commercially or made from 22-gauge wire

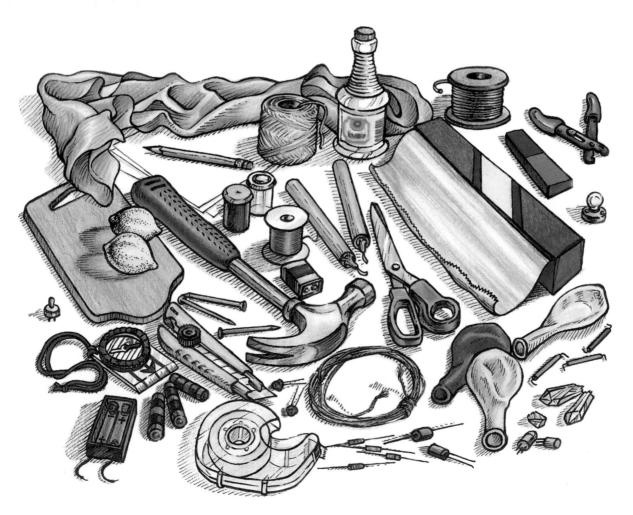

miniature light bulb (1.5 to 3 V) and light bulb holder, with connecting wires

miniature neon light bulb (from electronics supply store)

light-emitting diodes (LEDs)* (three)

wire:

- 20- to 24-gauge solid-core copper wire (insulated)
- 14 yards (13 m) of fine lacquered or varnished bell wire
- insulated bell wire
- picture-hanging wire
- 6 insulated copper wires with alligator clips at both ends, about 6 inches (15 cm) long or longer
- 8 feet (2.5 m) insulated copper wire

small electronic circuit board, also called a breadboard or socket board (about 300 holes), with letters and numbers

potentiometer*

resistors:* one 33-ohm, one 100-ohm, four 1000-ohm

toggle switches:* 2-way (on-off SPST); 3-way (SPDT)

wire strippers or cutters

strips of copper and zinc—6 of each metal; about ¼" (.5 cm) wide × 4 inches (10 cm)

electric or masking tape

OTHER SUPPLIES:

candles

aluminum foil

balloons

bar magnet

bottle of nail polish

coins

comb (plastic)

cork

craft knife

craft sticks (a few; the kind from ice cream pops)

doorknob (metal), attached to door

drinking straw (plastic)

drinking glass

eraser (rubber)

film canisters (transparent, from 35 mm film)

glass jars with lids (3)

hammer and nails, including small nails and a large iron nail, 3 or 4 inches long (8 to 10 cm)

kitchen knife

lemons (2) and other citrus fruit

metal coat hanger

metal foil (like the kind from chewing gum)

metal fork

model or craft glue

modeling clay

nylon stockings

paper and pencils, including wooden lead pencil

paper clips (large uncoated wire clips; small steel paper clips)

pie plates (disposable metal)

plastic drinking cup, 8 oz size

plastic pen

polystyrene (Styrofoam™) block and dinner plates

PVC tubing, about 3 feet (3 m) long

old vinyl record

potato

push pin

quartzite rocks and other assorted rocks

scissors

screw driver

soap bubble blower and bubble solution

string

thumb tacks

vinegar

water

wood: stick and piece the size of postcard

wool or silk fabric or piece of fur

woolen socks

Charging Forth

ATOMS AND CHARGES

Everything around you in the universe is made up of tiny particles called atoms. In fact, you are made up of atoms too. An atom is the smallest particle of a substance that still has all the qualities of that substance. Atoms are made of even smaller particles. In the center of each atom are particles called protons and neutrons. Whirling around the outside of each atom in cloudlike form are particles called electrons. Both elec-

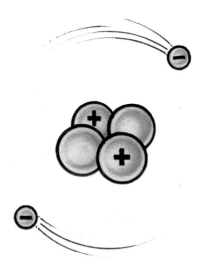

trons and protons have something called an electric charge. (Neutrons have no charge.) The charges on electrons and protons are of different types. Protons have a positive charge and electrons have a negative charge. Protons and electrons have charges of the same size. As the total number of protons in an atom is usually equal to the total number of electrons, the sum of the negative and positive charges is usually zero for an atom, and it is considered uncharged or neutral.

When an object or part of an object has unequal numbers of protons and electrons, we say that it is charged. This imbalance between protons and electrons is sometimes called charge separation, and it is the cause of static electricity. In this section, we'll repeat some early experiments with static electricity, and see what it can do. We'll also learn a little about lightning, an awesome example of what happens when a large static charge is discharged.

MORE ABOUT CHARGES

Transfer of Charges. Electrons can be transferred from one object to another. This makes the second object negatively charged, because it then has more electrons than protons. The first object is left with more protons than electrons and so is positively charged. This process is called separation of charge. The electrons aren't lost; they just move. When an object becomes negatively charged, another object must become positively charged by the same amount, because charges can't be created or destroyed. Electric charge is basic to all substances.

Opposites Attract; Same Charges Repel. Objects with positive charges are attracted to objects with negative charges. Objects with the same charge repel each other (push each other away). This is similar to what happens with the north poles of two magnets when they are brought close to each other.

Exciting Elektrons

The word "electricity" comes from the ancient Greek word elektron, which means amber. Amber is a brownish glassy material used to make jewelry. It is really fossilized tree sap that has hardened over

Photo 1. A piece of amber. If you look closely, you will see an insect embedded in it.

millions of years. The first recorded discovery of electricity occurred when Thales of Miletus (640–546 B.C.), an ancient Greek scientist and philosopher, rubbed a piece of amber with some fur to polish it. He noticed that the amber picked up small pieces of straw. He assumed that this was caused by an unknown force inside the amber. Using a plastic comb instead of amber, you can repeat his experiment. This is a perfect activity for a dry fall or winter day.

YOU WILL NEED

⇒ plastic comb
⇒ hair or a piece of fur or wool fabric
⇒ small pieces of paper or Styrofoam™
⇒ source of running water, such as a faucet

WHAT TO DO

Experiment 1

1. Comb your hair or rub the comb with a piece of fabric or fur. Move the comb out of your hair, but hold it about ½ inch (1 cm) away. Watch your hair.

2. When your hair starts to move towards the comb, hold the comb over the small pieces of paper or Styrofoam and watch what happens.

Photo 2. Charged comb attracting pieces of paper.

Experiment 2

1. Turn on the water tap so the water comes out in a thin, continuous stream.

2. Repeat Step 1 of Experiment 1; then hold the comb near the stream of water. Watch what happens to the stream of water.

Photo 3. Charged comb attracting a stream of water.

WHAT HAPPENED

As you combed your hair in Experiment 1, electrons moved from your hair to the comb. This left your hair with an excess of positive charges and the comb with an excess of negative charges. When you held the comb near your hair, your hair started to move towards the comb, because the comb and your hair were oppositely charged and were then attracted to each other. The negatively charged comb attracted the pieces of paper. The electrons in the paper moved away from the comb (because like charges repel each other), leaving the protons, with positive charge, in the area near the comb, surrounded with fewer electrons than usual. The negatively charged comb attracted the positive areas of the paper scraps. Once the paper touches the comb, it can become negatively charged, and you may have seen some of the pieces of paper jump back off the comb, as the papers were then repelled.

When the charged comb was brought near the running water in Experiment 2, the water was attracted to the comb, and seemed to bend out of its falling path. Water is made up

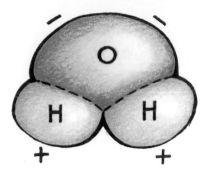

Water molecule showing location of partial charges. H = hydrogen. O = Oxygen.

of oxygen and hydrogen atoms that are joined together to form units called molecules. The electrons in water molecules can't be removed easily, but the oxygen side of each water molecule is more negative than the hydrogen side. The negatively charged comb attracted the more positively charged sides of the water molecules. Water molecules in the air on a damp day can make it difficult to see the effects of static electricity. In order to keep the charges separate, the air must act as an insulator (a substance that does not conduct a charge well). Damp air is not as good an insulator as dry air. If you find that your comb will not attract the little scraps of paper, you may need to make sure that the comb is really dry; maybe you will even have to heat the comb gently with a blow drier.

TRIBOELECTRIC* SEQUENCE

The substances we have been using (comb, fur, hair) don't let electrons travel through them easily. Another way of saying this is that they are poor conductors of electricity. One way of transferring electrons in poor conductors is by contact. Rubbing increases the area of contact. You can use the list below to tell how materials will become charged from being in contact with each other. A material that is higher on the list will become positively charged (lose electrons) if it is placed in contact with any substance that is lower on the list. Materials at the top of the list seem to lose electrons more easily than the ones lower down on the list. The farther apart two materials are on the list, the stronger the charge they can produce when brought into contact with each other.

1. rabbit fur
2. glass
3. nylon
4. wool
5. quartz
6. cat fur
7. lead
8. silk
9. paper
10. human skin, aluminum
11. cotton
12. wood
13. sealing wax
14. amber
15. polystyrene (Styrofoam™)
16. copper or brass
17. rubber balloon
18. sulfur
19. celluloid
20. hard rubber
21. plastic food wrap

*1 = most positive. 21 = most negative.

Versatile Versorium

In the 1500s, Queen Elizabeth I of England had a physician named William Gilbert. He was very interested in electricity and magnetism. He made a simple device he called a versorium to detect static electricity. It consisted of a piece of rigid lightweight nonmagnetic material, such as wood, which could turn easily on a pivot. Here is a quick and easy version of this static electricity detector, which you can make.

YOU WILL NEED

⇛ modeling clay
⇛ push pin
⇛ plastic drinking straw
⇛ scissors
⇛ plastic comb
⇛ person with hair, or a piece of fur or wool fabric
⇛ television set or computer monitor

WHAT TO DO

1. Roll a small piece of modeling clay into a small ball.

2. Push the flat end of the push pin into the ball of clay so that the point of the push pin is pointing straight out on top.

3. Use scissors to cut a 4 inch (10 cm) length of the drinking straw. Poke the point of the push pin through one side of the straw, exactly at the center of the straw. Ensure that the piece of straw can rotate around the point easily. This is your charge detector.

Photo 1. Finished versorium.

4. Charge the comb by combing it through your hair several times, or rub it with wool cloth or fur. Bring the comb near one end of the straw and watch what happens. Bring the comb near the other end of the straw and watch what happens (Photo 2).

Photo 2. Versorium attracted to charged comb.

5. Place the detector near the screen of a television set or computer monitor and watch what happens.

WHAT HAPPENED

When you rubbed the comb with wool or fur, or combed it through your hair, the comb gained electrons and became negatively charged. When the comb was placed near the straw, it caused the electrons on the end of the straw to move away, leaving behind a small positively charged region that was attracted to the comb, so the straw slowly moved towards the comb. When you placed the charged comb at the other end of the straw, the comb initially repelled the straw, as this second end of the straw was slightly negatively charged. The comb may then have attracted the straw, if it was negative enough to repel the negative charges at the second end of the straw, leaving the positive charges near the comb to be attracted. When the detector was placed near the screen of the television or computer monitor, it was attracted to the screen. There is a buildup of static charge on TV and computer monitors as they operate. This is why they get dusty so fast. The dust is attracted to the charge on the screen.

UNITS OF MEASUREMENT

As soon as people started studying electricity in a scientific way, they got interested in measuring things about it. The units we're using in this book to describe electricity are based on the International System of Units *(Le système internationale d'unités)* or SI. The SI is based on the metric system. The metric system uses multiples of 10 and uses a standard length of 1 metre and mass of 1 kilogram. Below are some units you'll come across in learning about electricity, and their abbreviations.

What It Measures	Unit Name	Abbreviation
mass	kilogram	kg
time	second	s
distance	metre	m
force	newton	N
work and energy	joule	J
power	watt	W
electric charge	coulomb	C
electric potential	volt	V
electric current	ampere	A
resistance	ohm	Ω
capacitance	farad	F

COULOMB

Charles Augustin de Coulomb (1736–1806) was a French physicist who investigated the size of electric charges and magnetic charges and how they acted over a distance. He demonstrated clearly that the force between two electrical charges is proportional to the product of the two forces. He also showed that as the distance between the objects increased, the force between them decreased with the square of the distance between them. (To find the square of a number, you multiply the number by itself. For example, the square of 3 is 3 x 3 or 9; the square of 5 is 25.)

In Coulomb's honor, the unit for electric charge is called the coulomb (C). One coulomb is about the same as the amount of charge going through a 100-watt light bulb to light it for 1 second.

Opposites Attract

You probably have done this at a birthday party. Little did you know that it was an experiment, and not simply a game.

YOU WILL NEED

⇒ 2 balloons
⇒ two 2-foot (60 cm) pieces of string
⇒ silk scarf, nylon stocking, wool sock, or sweater
⇒ soap bubble blower and soap bubble solution

WHAT TO DO

Blow up the balloons and tie a piece of string to the end of each balloon.

Experiment 1

Hold a balloon in your right hand and rub the balloon with the nylon stocking with your left hand. Still holding the nylon, take your right hand off the balloon (Photo 1). Where did the balloon go to? Try this again, this time using other fabrics. Is the result the same each time?

Experiment 2

Rub both balloons with the nylon stocking. Hold the strings of both balloons in one hand and lift the balloons off the table. What do the balloons do?

Photo 2. Suspended balloons repelling each other (Experiment 2).

Photo 1. Charging a balloon by rubbing with a nylon.

Experiment 3

Rub one balloon against your hair. Place that balloon close to a wall. Does it stick? Did you hear any noise? What did your hair do as you rubbed the balloon against it?

Photo 3. Charged balloon attracting hair (Experiment 3).

Photo 4. Charged balloon sticking to a wall (Experiment 3).

Experiment 4

Try this activity outside on a sunny day with little wind. Rub a balloon as you did in the above experiments. Have a friend blow soap bubbles into the air, and hold your balloon close to a bubble. What happens to the bubble?

WHAT HAPPENED

In Experiment 1, you found that when you let go of the balloon, it was attracted to the nylon. When you rubbed the balloon with the nylon, electrons were transferred from the nylon to the balloon, which became negatively charged. The nylon was positively charged because it lost electrons. Opposite charges attract each other, so the balloon was attracted to the nylon. The same thing happened when the balloon came near the soap bubbles (Experiment 4). The bubbles are neutral; they have an equal number of positive and negative charges, but they were attracted to the negatively charged balloon because the electrons in the balloon repelled the negative charges in the soap bubbles and attracted the positive charges that remained in the area near the balloon.

In Experiment 2, when both the balloons were rubbed with nylon, both were negatively charged. They moved away from each other because like charges repel each other (Photo 2).

In Experiment 3, when the balloon was rubbed against your hair, electrons from your hair moved to the balloon and the balloon became negatively charged (Photo 3). When you placed the balloon near the wall, it repelled the electrons in a small area of the wall and became attracted to the part of the wall that was now positively charged. This allowed the balloon to stick to the wall (Photo 4). The crackling you may have heard from the charged balloon was caused by some of the electrons jumping through the air back onto your hair from the balloon as the charge in the balloon became quite large. When this happened, you hair may have stood on end, as it was all negatively charged and the pieces of hair repelled each other because they had the same charge.

Thor's Hammer

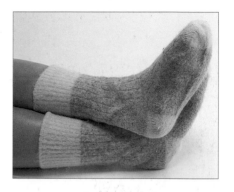

People in ancient times imagined that the lightning that streaked across the sky was created by an angry god. When the lightning bolt struck an object, such as a tree or a building, surely this was a message from on high. Thor was the mythological god of thunder, and was thought of as the strongest of all the Norse gods. One of the days of the week is named after him—Thursday (Thor's day). Today we know that lightning is a giant example of an electric discharge. Here is an experiment to create your own safe bolt of "lightning."

YOU WILL NEED

⇒ wool socks

⇒ carpet of nylon or other synthetic material

⇒ metal doorknob

⇒ nylon stockings, wool sweater, or silk scarf

WHAT TO DO

Experiment 1

Put on a pair of thick wool socks and run around the room, dragging your feet on the carpet. Point your finger about an inch away from a metal doorknob and watch what happens! Shocking, isn't it? You can try this on an unsuspecting friend, but be prepared for an all-out static fight as your friend gets even with you. Warning: do not do this to your pet cat, as cats tend to fight back, using claws!

Experiment 2

In a dark room with the lights turned off, stand in front of a mirror holding a nylon stocking. Rub the stocking together and watch your reflection in the mirror. What do you see?

Try this again, this time using different materials such as a wool sweater or a silk scarf.

WHAT HAPPENED

In both experiments, you produced an electric discharge. In Experiment 1, electrons were transferred between your socks and the carpet, so you became electrically charged. When your finger came near the doorknob, the electrons passed between your finger and the doorknob (which is a conductor), through the air, causing a spark. In Experiment 2, sparks flew back and forth between parts of the nylon stocking as electrons moved back and forth, giving small static charges to different areas of the nylons.

Lightning

Lightning happens because particles within a cloud become charged and tend to separate into positive ones at the upper portion and negative ones at the bottom of the cloud. The separation of charges creates enormous electrical potential, which can be millions of volts. Finally, when the charge is large enough, the separation of charges breaks down and a flash begins. Lightning is an electrical discharge between positive and negative regions of storm clouds, or between the clouds and the ground. Lightning can go from cloud to ground, from the ground to the clouds, or from one part of a cloud to another.

BEN FRANKLIN

Benjamin Franklin made the first systematic study of lightning and proved that lightning was a form of electricity. He did this when he flew a kite with a metal rod attached to the top in a thunderstorm. He tied one end of a twine string to the kite and the other end to a metal key. He then tied a silk ribbon to the same key and held the other end of the silk ribbon. Franklin was smart enough to get out of the rain, and stood someplace dry, holding the end of the silk ribbon.

Most books say that a bolt of lightning struck the metal rod, sending a rush of electrons down the wet twine and striking the key. Some sources say that Franklin held his hand near the key and saw a spark travel between the two, while other sources say that the string ended in a container called a Leyden jar, which can store an electrical charge. In fact, the kite may not have been struck by lightning at all, as this would have surely killed Franklin. It is likely that the kite and string merely became electrified as they collected bits of charge from the air. The twine was only slightly conductive and in turn electri-

fied the key, but did not conduct enough of a charge down the line to harm old Ben. Franklin was lucky he wasn't killed! Others have tried to repeat this experiment and have died trying.

LIGHTNING SAFETY

1. Do not stay outdoors in a thunderstorm. Go inside.
2. If you cannot make it safely inside, do not stand under a tree for shelter. Crouch down as low to the ground as you can, but don't lie down.
3. Stay away from water. Get out of a pool or lake.
4. Do not sit on metal bleachers, or stand near a telephone pole or on a hillside during a thunderstorm. Do not hold any metal objects, even a baseball bat or bicycle, if lightning is nearby.
5. It is alright to sit in a car during a storm because even if the car is struck, the metal frame carries the charge around you. Keep the win-

dows rolled up and don't touch any part of the exterior of the car.
6. Turn off the computer and television during a storm. Lightning has been known to harm these devices. Don't use the telephone if the lightning flashes are close by.
7. Do not fly a kite during a thunderstorm.

ELVES

Elves exist. We don't mean magical creatures or wee folk. In scientific terms, an elve is a large horizontal brightening of several hundred miles across the ionosphere (upper atmosphere) directly above an active thunderstorm. Videos shot from the Space Shuttle from 1989 to 1991 were the first proof of these optical flashes. There are other kinds of brief brightenings over thunderstorms, including sprites and blue jets. If you are interested in learning more about this subject, various scientists studying these occurrences have Web sites showing their research. You can also go to the

NASA Web site and use the word "lightning" or "sprites" to search for information there.

FULGURITES

What happens when lightning strikes the earth? In most cases, the earth absorbs the charge and the ground around the strike remains unchanged. However, sometimes when lightning strikes sand high in the mineral silica, something really unusual happens: the heat of the lightning causes the sand to melt and fuse together. This creates glasslike hollow tubes called sand fulgurites. Fulgurites get their name from the Latin word fulgur, or lightning. These fragile tubes can be found just below the surface of the sand. The outside of a fulgurite is rough and covered with bits of quartz sand, while the inside is smooth and glassy. If you were to try to make a fulgurite, you would have to heat silica sand to over 2950°F (1620°C)! In very rare instances, fulgurites are formed when lightning hits soil or rock which contains a large amount of silica.

Red sprite above a thunderstorm, Arkansas. Courtesy of Dr. Davis D. Sentman, Geophysical Institute, University of Alaska, Fairbanks.

Sparkling Personality

The first experiment with electricity was not recorded. It happened when a cave dweller discovered, perhaps by accident, that when certain kinds of rocks were struck together, they produced sparks. Sparks lit tiny pieces of wood or leaves, and created a fire. This early scientist did not say, "Hey, cool! I've made a piezoelectric charge." He had better things to do, like learning to walk erect and avoiding creatures that wanted to dine on him. See if you can get a spark using the same tools as your ancient ancestors did!

YOU WILL NEED

⇒ two piezoelectric rocks*
⇒ other kinds of rocks

WHAT TO DO

1. Close the blinds or shades in a room so no light comes in.

2. Stand in front of a mirror. Have a friend turn off all the lights in the room.

3. Bang the two piezoelectric rocks together (or ones you think might be). Watch your reflection in the mirror and see if you made any flashes inside the rocks. Turn on the lights and let your friend have a try. Do different ways of banging the rocks together make larger flashes?

4. Now try the same thing with

Photo 1. Piezoelectric rocks. A chunk of quartz and a single quartz crystal on the left, tourmaline in the center, and rose quartz, unpolished and polished, on the right.

*You can purchase piezoelectric rocks at specialty toy stores or museum shops. You can use pieces of quartz, quartzite or tourmaline, which can be purchased at a lapidary shop; quartz can be found on the ground in most places. Many of the smooth white rocks you find at the beach are quartzite. If you find a white rock at the beach and it doesn't bubble when placed in vinegar, it is probably quartzite. Ask permission before banging together any valuable rocks, as they can be chipped and cracked.

your other rock samples. Can you produce sparks? Label the ones that cause flashes.

WHAT HAPPENED

Your piezoelectric rocks produced a small spark when struck together. If you strike them harder, the flashes will be brighter. This type of light production from striking is called triboluminescence. Other rocks won't produce the same kind of spark, unless they are also piezoelectric. Piezoelectricity

Photo 2. Quartzite rock also can be used to create sparks.

means electricity from pressure. (*Piezein* means "press" in Greek.) Organized scientific study of piezoelectricity began

in 1880 when two brothers, Pierre and Jacques Curie, discovered it in quartz and Rochelle salt. These French scientists found that when a piezoelectric crystal was squeezed, it produced an electric potential or voltage across the face of the crystal. (The reverse is true also: if an electric potential is applied across the face of the crystal, it causes the crystal to change shape.) This ability to convert pressure to electricity and back was later used in devices such as microphones and watches.

Falling Leaves

You have already seen a very simple device for detecting static electric charges in Versatile Versorium. Here is a more sophisticated device which you can use to learn about the different ways these charges can be transferred. This device is called a metal-leaf electroscope. One way to remember the name is that an electroscope is something that detects or "scopes out" charges.

YOU WILL NEED

⇒ small glass jar with a
   metal lid
⇒ thin nail and hammer
⇒ metal coat hanger
⇒ wire cutters
⇒ modeling clay
⇒ piece of foil
⇒ thin foil wrapper from a
   candy bar or gum
⇒ scissors
⇒ plastic comb
⇒ wool or silk fabric

WHAT TO DO

1. Have an adult use the hammer to drive the nail through the lid of the jar. When this is done, have the adult cut a 6 inch (15 cm) piece of coat hanger wire and bend one end of wire ½ inch (1 cm) at a right angle to the rest of the wire. Slide the unbent end of the wire through the hole in the lid so the bent end is toward the inside of the lid, and secure the wire on top of the lid with modeling clay.

2. Remove any paper from the thin foil wrapper and cut it into a ½ × 3 inch (1 cm × 7.5 cm) strip.

3. Drop the foil onto the bend in the wire. Then place the lid on the jar.

4. Crumple a small piece of foil into a ball and carefully place this on the top of the wire. Make sure the foil stays on the wire.

5. Rub the comb with the fabric to create a charge; then gently touch the foil ball with the comb (Photo 1, Diagram 1). Look at the foil strip.

6. Touch the foil ball with your finger gently.

7. Charge the comb again by rubbing it with fabric. Hold the charged comb close to the metal foil ball. Without moving the comb, touch the foil ball at the top of your electroscope with your finger. Look at the metal strips again (Photo 2, Diagram 2).

WHAT HAPPENED

You made a metal leaf electroscope. It detects charges. The foil leaves are connected by a conductor to the metal foil ball outside the jar, but insulated from the jar itself. When you rubbed the plastic comb with the fabric (Step 5), you gave the comb a negative charge, or an excess of electrons. When you touched the foil ball with the charged comb, the electrons were transferred from the comb to the foil, and the electroscope

Photo 1. Charging by conduction.

Diagram 1. Charging by conduction. Negatively charged leaves of electroscope repel each other and move apart.

had a negative charge. When a charged object touches another object and transfers its charge, it is called charging by conduction. The electrons stay in the foil because the glass of the jar acts as an insulator. It stops the electrons from moving out of the foil. The two sides of the

Photo 2. Charging by induction (from comb), with grounding (finger).

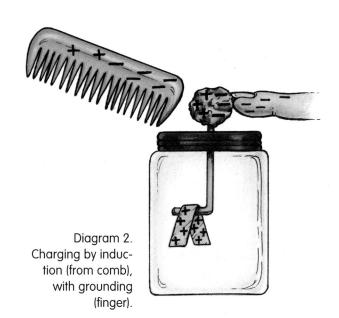

Diagram 2. Charging by induction (from comb), with grounding (finger).

foil strip have the same negative charge, so they repel each other, because like charges repel.

When you touched the foil ball with your finger in Step 6, you allowed the electrons to move from the foil into your finger. The foil ball was "grounded" by your finger and body, which are large and could act as a reservoir for the charge. This made the foil neutral or uncharged, and the strips fell back together. The number of positive and negative charges in the foil are the same in the neutral foil.

When you placed the negatively charged comb near the foil ball (but not touching it) in Step 7, the negative charges in the foil ball were pushed away from the comb, forming a negatively and positively charged region in the ball. When an object gets an electric charge from a charged object without touching it, the process is called charging by induction.

The negative charges in the foil ball were pushed away from the comb. When you touched the foil ball with your finger, you allowed some of the electrons in the foil to move up out of the electroscope into your body. This left the electroscope foil leaves with fewer negative charges than positive ones, and an overall positive charge resulted. This made the leaves both positively charged and the leaves moved apart again.

Sparkling Lights

When you plug a fluorescent or neon light into a power source, it lights up. But what if we told you that you can make it light up another way? Find out how and make your own static detector in this project.

YOU WILL NEED

⇒ small clear plastic film canister (from 35 mm film) with lid
⇒ hammer and nail
⇒ miniature neon light bulb (from electronic supply store)
⇒ glue
⇒ aluminum foil
⇒ scissors
⇒ book
⇒ small block of polystyrene (Styrofoam™)
⇒ wool fabric, plastic wrap, or rug
⇒ television or radio

WHAT TO DO

1. Have an adult use a nail to poke a hole through the middle of both the lid and bottom of the canister. There is a small indentation where the holes should go (Photo 1).

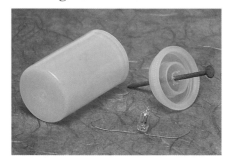

Photo 1. Canister and lid with holes, and nail and neon bulb with wires bent.

2. Gently bend the neon light bulb's wires flat. Insert one wire into the hole in the bottom of the canister and the other end through the lid of the canister. This is tricky and may take several attempts. When you've done this, cap the canister and flatten the wires against the canister so they stay in place (Photo 2).

Photo 2. Finished detector.

3. Place a thin line of glue around the rim of canister on both the top and bottom, making sure that glue does not touch the wires. Place a small round piece of foil on top of the glue on both the top and bottom of the canister so that each of the pieces of foil covers one end of the canister. You may wish to place a heavy book on top of the canister while the glue is drying, to ensure that the foil stays in place. This is your detector.

4. Take the detector into a darkened room. Rub the polystyrene block against a wool sweater, rug, or even the cat to get a static charge. Touch the detector to the polystyrene block and observe what happens.

5. Use your static detector to test your television screen or radio by touching the detector to the screen. Which produces the most static charge?

WHAT HAPPENED

The polystyrene block gained extra electrons from being rubbed by the fabric. When the detector was touched with the charged block, electrons moved into the neon bulb from the foil, and the light glowed. Inside a neon light is neon gas. When the extra electrons from the charged block make the atoms of neon gas move around and bump into each other, the gas atoms become excited and give off light. When you touch the TV screen or the radio with your detector, it may also light up. The brightness of the light bulb is an indication of the size of the static charge on the TV screen or radio.

You can try a similar experiment by rubbing an unattached fluorescent light bulb (one not in a circuit) with a piece of plastic wrap. Fluorescent light bulbs have special chemical coating inside, as well as mercury and argon gas. When the argon gas atoms get excited by the electrons, they collide with the mercury gas atoms, which causes the mercury gas to gain energy. The mercury gas gives off this extra energy as ultraviolet light. This affects the bulb's coating of chemicals, causing it to give off visible light.

Sparks Will Fly

An electrophorus is a device that collects and holds charges of static electricity and can be used to transfer charges. It will really give you the kind of spark that you can see and hear! This device was first made in 1775 by Italian scientist Alessandro Volta. (See Nuts and Volts to learn more about Volta.)

YOU WILL NEED

⇒ short, thick candle

⇒ match

⇒ metal pie plate or large, smooth metal lid like one from an old paint can (do not use a sharp lid)

⇒ thumb tack (optional)

⇒ Styrofoam plate or old vinyl record

⇒ piece of wool or silk fabric

WHAT TO DO

1. Have an adult light the candle, and drip wax into the center of the pie plate. When there is a large blob, blow out the candle and press the unmelted, flat end firmly into the liquid wax (Photo 1). **Note:** If you really want it to hold, you can stick a thumbtack through from the bottom of the plate into the base of the candle.

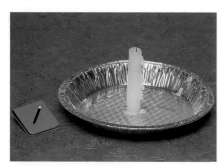

Photo 1. Metal pie plate with melted wax and candle attached.

2. Rub the surface of the Styrofoam plate or old record with a piece of wool or silk to transfer a negative charge to the plate (Photo 2).

Photo 2. Styrofoam plate being charged by rubbing with fabric.

3. Holding the pie plate by the candle handle, place the plate on top of the charged Styrofoam plate.

4. Briefly touch the pie plate with your finger, or get a friend to do this (Photo 3).

Photo 3. Charge being transferred to the metal plate.

5. Using the handle, remove the pie plate from the charged surface. Use it in the next

experiment, or test it using the static detector from Sparkling Lights.

WHAT HAPPENED

You made an electrophorus. In Step 2, you gave the Styrofoam plate or record a negative charge by transferring electrons to the plate (or record) from the fabric by rubbing. In Step 3, when you placed the metal plate on top of the negatively charged Styrofoam plate, the negative charges in the foil plate moved away from the Styrofoam plate. When you touched the metal plate with your finger, you removed these electrons. When you touched the metal plate with your finger in Step 4, you probably felt a small shock as the electrons were transferred to your body from the metal plate, leaving you with a negative charge. If you do this in the dark, you may even see a small spark between the metal plate and your finger. You can't see the charge you have built up, as this electric charge is invisible, but you can take your electrophorus and carry it somewhere to do the next experiment. In the next experiment you will be able to see if there is a charge when you try to transfer it, or you can test for the charge using the detector.

VAN DE GRAAFF GENERATOR

With a charged balloon, you can get some of your hair to stand on end. Using a device called a Van de Graaff generator is a sure way to get even more of your hair to look like a porcupine's quills. This device was named after its inventor, Robert J. Van de Graaff, who invented it in 1931. If you could look inside a Van de Graaff generator, you would see that it has a long rubber belt running from the top of the ball down through a metal tube, and connecting to a motor on the bottom. There is a charge-spraying device next to the motor and a charge collector at the top. As the belt turns, it picks up electrons from the charge sprayer and carries them to the charge collector at the top and onto the ball.

When you touch the ball, the electrons move into your body and out to the ends of your hair. Because all the tips of your hair have the same charge, they repel each other, and your hair stands on end.

What's Your Capacity?

As you know from the previous experiment, a static charge doesn't last very long. No matter how much of a charge you build up with the electrophorus, unless you have someplace to store it, the charge will be transferred the first time it touches something else. Is it possible to save a static charge? Yes. You can use something called a Leyden jar. A Leyden jar is one of a group of devices called capacitors or condensers. A capacitor is something that holds a charge. One of the first Leyden jars was made in 1745 at the University of Leyden in Holland. Try making this small version of the Leyden jar.

Warning: *Do not do this experiment if you have a pacemaker or heart problems.*

YOU WILL NEED

⇒ empty 35 mm film canister
⇒ 2 inch (5 cm) nail and hammer
⇒ scissors
⇒ aluminum foil
⇒ picture-hanging wire
⇒ water
⇒ charging apparatus (electrophorus) from Sparks Will Fly

WHAT TO DO

1. Have an adult hammer the nail through the center of the top of the lid of the film canister. The nail should be firmly seated in the lid with about ½ inch (1 cm) of the top of the nail sticking out of the top of the lid (see Photo 1).

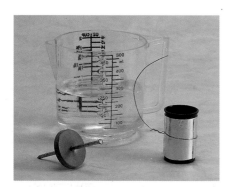

Photo 1. Lid with nail stuck through hole, and film canister with foil and wire around it.

2. Cut a piece of foil 1½ inches by 5 inches (3.5 cm by 12.5 cm). Wrap the piece of foil around the outside of the canister.

3. Cut an 8 inch (20 cm) piece of wire, and wrap it around the outside of the canister. Twist the ends together to secure the wire, leaving a piece of wire long enough to touch the top of the nail when the lid is in place.

4. Half-fill the film canister with tap water. The nail must touch the water when the lid is in place. Place the lid on the canister. This is your Leyden jar.

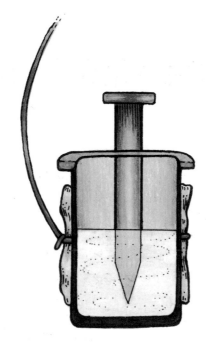

Diagram 1. Completed Leyden jar, showing both inside and outside parts in cross section.

5. Take the charged pie plate from the Sparks Will Fly experiment and touch it to the top of the nail on the lid of the Leyden jar. Recharge the plate and repeat several times (Photo 2).

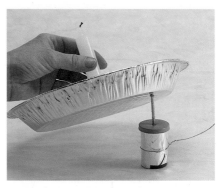

Photo 2. Completed Leyden jar being charged.

6. Here is the neat part: Hold the foil on the outside of the canister with your left hand and place a finger from your right hand just over the nail (Photo 3).

Photo 3. Completed jar being discharged.

7. Try charging the Leyden jar again with the charged pie plate; then move the loose end of the wire near the head of the nail without touching it, and watch what happens. If you can't see anything, try it in the dark.

WHAT HAPPENED

Basically, a capacitor consists of 2 pieces of material that conduct electricity (in this case the nail and the foil) that are near each other, but not touching. They are separated by a substance that doesn't conduct electricity, called an insulator (in this case, the film canister). One plate of the capacitor receives the charge, but it can't go anywhere until there is a path for the electrons to flow from one plate to the other.

In Step 5, when you touched the positively charged plate to the nail of the Leyden jar, electrons were transferred from the nail and the water inside of the jar to the charged pie plate. (Water is a conductor as well as the nail.) This left the Leyden jar with a positive charge. Because you were able to transfer charges several times to the pie plate, you were able to store a large charge in the jar. In Step 6, when you held your hand near the nail on the jar and touched the foil, you connected the inside and the outside of the jar with your body, and you felt a tingle, as electrons flowed from your body into the jar. In the dark, you may have seen a small spark as electrons jumped from your fingers to the nail. To learn more about capacitors, see Flash a Smile.

Coming Down the Pipe

There is the classic way to make an electrophorus; then there is the really complicated version of a static generator such as the Van de Graaff generator, which you may have seen on television or in a science center, but is there anything in between? Now there is. You can make your own manual static electricity generator with some household items.

YOU WILL NEED

⇒ 3-foot (90 cm) piece of thin PVC pipe
⇒ piece of fur, wool, or silk cloth
⇒ Nine 6-inch (15 cm) pieces of picture wire
⇒ Leyden jar from What's Your Capacity?

WHAT TO DO

1. Create a "bundle" by wrapping a piece of picture wire around the middle of the other eight pieces of wire. Leave a loose end on the wrapping piece and bend the other wires in half in a "U". These are your pickup wires. Attach the loose end of the tying wire to the nail of the Leyden jar. Bend the wire on the side of the Leyden jar so the end of the wire is about ¼ inch (0.4 cm) from the top of the nail (see Photo 1).

2. Wrap fur or cloth around one end of the PVC pipe.

3. Hold the pipe so that it is really close to the ends of the wire bundles.

4. Stroke the pipe by pushing the fabric along the length of the pipe (Photo 2).

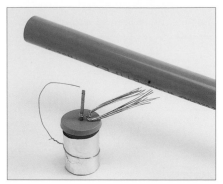

Photo 1. Setup with Leyden jar.

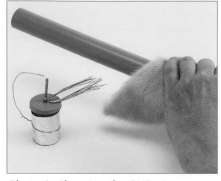

Photo 2. Charging the PVC pipe.

5. Look at the space between the top of the nail and the wire from the side of the Leyden jar.

WHAT HAPPENED

When you rubbed the PVC tubing with the cloth, you transferred electrons from the cloth to the tubing. Because the tubing was quite long, you had a large surface to work with and you were able to build up a fairly large charge. When the charge became large enough, the electrons jumped the gap to the ends of the pickup wires. The Leyden jar became charged. When there was enough charge inside the jar, it discharged from the nail head through the air to the wire on the side of the jar, and you saw a spark.

OTTO VON GUERICKE

Otto von Guericke was the mayor of the town of Magdeburg in Germany in the mid 17th century. He was very curious about the world around him and performed many different types of experiments. In 1672 von Guericke invented a machine which allowed him to gather a large static charge easily. His device consisted of a hollow glass globe, which he turned with a crank. Inside the globe, he placed a ball of sulfur. Near the outside of the globe, he placed two small brushes with metal rods attached. On the tips of the metal rods there were small metal balls. When the crank was turned and von Guericke held a cloth against the sphere, it became negatively charged. As soon as there were enough extra electrons, they were picked up by the brushes. The charge on the brushes eventually built up until there were too many electrons; then the electrons began to jump across the space between the two metal balls, causing sparks to fly.

Swift Current

P A R T 2

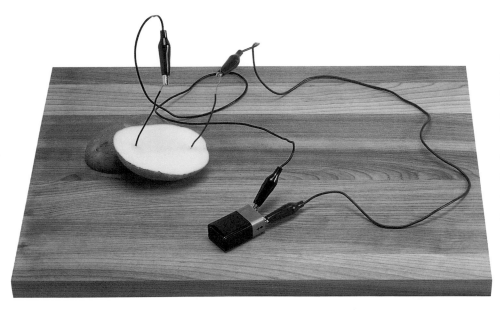

conductive material is called an electric current. Electric current is measured in amperes. What other types of charged particles besides electrons move to make electric currents? Sometimes atoms or groups of atoms lose or gain one or more electrons, so become positively or negatively charged. They are called ions. Ions can travel through liquids such as water to cause electric currents. In this section, we'll learn more about electric currents.

The first section of this book looked at static charges. We studied different aspects of charge separation. We worked with some things that didn't conduct electricity well, like glass and rubber. They are called insulators. In this section of the book, we are going to look at the flow or movement of electrons or other charged particles through things that do conduct electricity well.

Electrons in metals such as copper or silver act in an interesting way. The protons and neutrons that form the nuclei of these metals' atoms are locked in position. The electrons are loosely held and can move from atom to atom fairly easily. We say that copper and silver are good conductors because they allow electrons to move through them easily. The flow of electrons through a wire or other

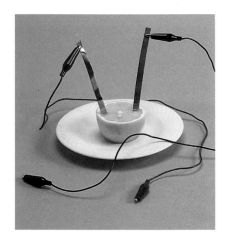

Nuts and Volts

Are you so active that your parents think you ought to have a unit of electricity named after you? This happened to many of the scientists who made discoveries in the field of electricity, including Alessandro Volta. Let's see why.

YOU WILL NEED

⇒ vinegar

⇒ 3 glass jars or cups

⇒ 3 strips of copper, about ¼ inch × 4 inches (0.5 cm × 10 cm). You can use strips of copper sheeting or copper pipe

⇒ 3 strips of zinc, ¼ inch × 4 inches (.5 cm × 10 cm), available at hardware stores

⇒ 4 pieces of insulated wire with alligator clips at both ends of each

⇒ LED (light-emitting diode)*

⇒ modeling clay (optional)

WHAT TO DO

1. Half-fill each glass jar with vinegar.

2. Place a strip of copper in each of the glass jars. Place a strip of zinc in each of the glass jars. Make sure that the two strips of metal are not touching each other. You can use a piece

*An LED is an electrical device that gives off light when electric current passes through it. Note: The longer leg of the LED is the positive (+) terminal.

of modeling clay in the bottom of the jar to hold the metal strips in place, if necessary (Photo 1). See Photo 2 for Steps 3 to 6.

3. Take wire 1 and attach it with the alligator clip to the positive terminal (the longer wire) of the LED. Attach the other end of wire 1 to the piece of copper in the first jar.

4. Attach the second alligator clip wire to the strip of zinc in the first jar and the other end of this wire to the strip of copper in the second jar.

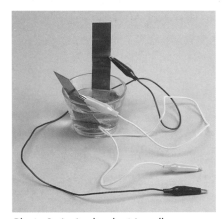

Photo 1. A single electric cell.

5. Attach the third wire to the strip of zinc in the second jar and the other end of this wire to the strip of copper in the third jar.

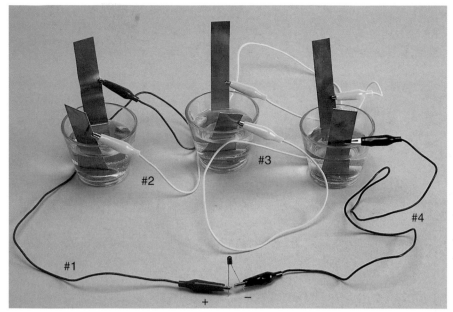

Photo 2. A three-cell battery with an LED.

Some of the zinc atoms in the zinc strip changed into ions by releasing electrons into the wire. The electrons traveled through the wire and entered the copper strip, which was the positive terminal. At the same time, positive zinc ions moved through the vinegar, which acted as the electrolyte. What caused the electrons and ions to move is that the two metals have different electric potentials. The difference in potential between two points in a circuit is called the voltage, and it is measured in units called volts. Each of the pairs of metal strips in the jars produces about 1 volt. Connecting the metals in the three jars together increased the total electric potential to about 3 volts, so there was enough of an electric potential to light up the LED.

6. Take the fourth piece of wire and attach it with the alligator clip to the negative terminal (the one with the shorter wire) of the LED. Attach the other end of the wire to the strip of zinc in the third jar.

WHAT HAPPENED

You made a battery. A battery is a group of electric cells. Each cup with its 2 strips of metal is an electric cell in which the zinc is the negative electrode.

DID YOU KNOW?

What do you think is the closest electric current to you? You don't have to look far. The closest electric current is in your body. Moving ions in your body cause electric currents in your brain and nerves. Doctors use the electric currents in your body to see how your heart is working, using a device called an electrocardiograph, which produces a tracing called an electrocardiogram. Each time your heart beats, there are changes in its electrical potential. These changes can be measured using small metal contacts or electrodes, which are placed on a layer of electrolyte gel on your skin. The electrodes are placed in different areas and the potential differences between these areas are measured. Tracings are made for several heartbeats. An experienced doctor can tell if your heart is damaged by looking at the shape of the tracings.

GALVANI AND VOLTA

You have heard of animal magnetism, but have you ever heard of animal electricity? One of the most interesting discoveries in the history of electricity was made by Luigi Galvani (1737–1798), a professor of anatomy at the University of Bologna, Italy, who studied nerves and muscles using frogs. Galvani attached small metal hooks to the muscles in a dead frog's legs. He then put electricity from a static electricity machine through the muscle to look at the contraction (shortening) of the muscle. One day he noticed that the muscle would contract without the static electricity machine if the metals touching it were two different metals. He tried this with several different metals and found they had the same effect. He thought he had discovered a source of "animal electricity," which might explain how living things were able to be alive.

Alessandro Volta (1745–1827) was a professor of natural history at the University of Pavia, Italy, who had made several important discoveries about electricity. The electrophorus was one of his earliest inventions. He heard about Galvani's discovery. Volta thought that perhaps the electricity was not caused by the frog's nerves or muscles or "animal electricity," but instead was related to the metals attached to the frog's legs in Galvani's experiments. Around 1794, Volta invented the voltaic pile, a device to test his ideas. He placed discs of zinc and silver together; between them, he placed pieces of cloth or paper soaked in salt water or acid. He constructed a pile of these discs and found that when strips of metal attached to the ends of the pile were brought together, sparks flew! Unlike the Leyden jar, the pile did not lose its charge, but supplied a continuous source of electric charge. Volta had invented the first electric battery.

Volta called the type of battery which we made in Nuts and Volts a "crown of cups." He first published his results about the voltaic pile in 1800. For Volta's distinguished career, Napoleon Bonaparte of France made him a count and awarded him other honors. His invention gave other scientists a powerful tool for studying electricity. The volt was named to honor him.

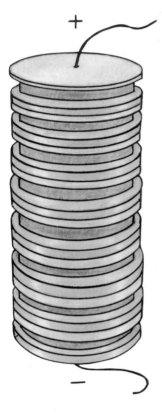

Diagram 1. Volta's pile. The discs were made of silver and zinc, separated by paper soaked in salt water.

Lemon Light

What do you think lemons, potatoes, and coins have to do with electricity? As it turns out, they are all things you can use to cause an electric charge to flow. From these materials you can discover how a battery works. Lemons are wonderful fruit! They make great summer drinks. They add flavor to cooked fish. They contain essential vitamins. They can turn on a light bulb. Wait! Did you say "turn on a light bulb"? No way.... Yes, there is a way.

YOU WILL NEED

⇒ 2 ripe, juicy lemons
⇒ 2 ripe, juicy oranges, limes, or grapefruit
⇒ knife
⇒ 3 strips of copper ¼ inch × 4 inches (0.5 cm × 10 cm)
⇒ 3 strips of zinc ¼ inch × 4 inches (0.5 cm × 10 cm)
⇒ 4 pieces of insulated wire with alligator clips at both ends
⇒ LED (light-emitting diode)

WHAT TO DO

1. Have an adult cut two lemons in half. Using only half of a lemon, insert the strip of copper in one side of the lemon and the zinc strip in the other side (see Photo 1). Make sure

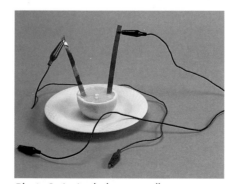

Photo 1. A single lemon cell.

the metals are inserted into the juicy part and not into the white, pulpy part of the fruit. The tops of these strips are your terminals.

2. Attach one end of the first wire with an alligator clip to the copper terminal. Attach one end of the second wire with an alligator clip to the zinc terminal (Photo 1).

3. Attach the loose end of the first wire from the copper strip to the long leg (positive terminal) of the LED. Attach the loose end of the wire from the zinc strip to the shorter leg of the LED. What happens?

4. Place copper and zinc strips in two more lemon halves and put them next to the first lemon. Remove the alligator clip on the zinc terminal from the LED and connect it to the second lemon's copper terminal. Then connect the zinc terminal of the second lemon half to the copper terminal in the third lemon half using wire 3 with alligator clips. Using wire 4 with alligator clips, attach the free (negative) leg of the LED to the zinc strip in the third lemon (see Photo 2). What happens?

5. If you wish, you can use other citrus fruits, such as oranges, grapefruit or limes. Which fruit works the best?

WHAT HAPPENED

When you connected the wires to the LED and to the metals in the three lemons, the LED lit up. The lemon half with the zinc and copper strips in it is an electrochemical cell. When two or more cells are connected together, we call them a battery. All cells or batteries have a negative electrode or terminal. In your cell, this was the strip of zinc. Cells also have a positive electrode or terminal — in this case, the piece of copper. Zinc loses electrons more easily than copper. The acidic lemon juice acted as the electrolyte, or conducting solution. Electrolytes contain charged particles called ions, which can move between the electrodes. Acids are good electrolytes because they form ions in water solutions. These chemical changes act like an

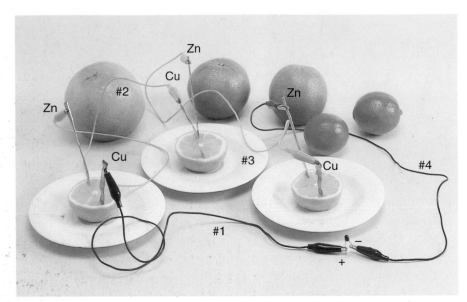

Photo 2. A lemon battery attached to an LED. Cu = copper, Zn = zinc.

"electron pump" to push the electrons through the wire, so that an electric current is produced. If you look at the electrodes after a while, you will see that some of the zinc looks like it has been eaten away, and that there are small bubbles around the copper. Zinc changes to zinc ions, which dissolve. The bubbles around the copper are hydrogen gas, separated from the electrolyte.

Each cell alone produced a small amount of electric potential or voltage (see Nuts and Volts), but not enough to light the LED. When you connected the three lemons together, you saw that the LED lit. Because you connected the lemons together in series, you increased the overall voltage, allowing the LED to light. Lemons tend to make better batteries and electrochemical cells than most other fruits because they have more acid. The lemon cell you made produces about 0.7 volts.

FUEL CELLS

Even though batteries have been around since about 1794, innovations continue to occur. One area of new technology is in the design of a special type of electrochemical cell called a fuel cell. Fuel cells are batteries in which chemicals are continuously added so that the battery can't run down and stop working. A company called Ballard Power Systems, Inc., in Vancouver, B.C., Canada makes fuel cells which use hydrogen gas and oxygen gas to produce electricity. The two gases are separated by a special thin membrane. When the cells are connected to make batteries, they are strong enough to use to move cars, buses or even submarines! Fuel cells have also been used in outer space on the Gemini space mission and on the Space Shuttle. The waste product of these batteries is warm water. Several automobile com-

panies have ordered these cells for use in battery-operated cars. These cars will be able to travel longer distances than earlier battery operated cars and would produce much less pollution than standard gasoline-burning automobiles.

Circuit Conductors

Not everything conducts or allows electricity to pass through it equally well. Some materials are better conductors than others. Let's test some things to learn more. See if you can predict which household items will allow the light to turn on, when connected to the battery and wires.

YOU WILL NEED

⇒ paper and pen or pencil
⇒ 3 wires with alligator clips at each end
⇒ 1.5 to 3 volt buzzer
⇒ LED (light-emitting diode)
⇒ holder for 2 AA batteries
⇒ 2 AA batteries
⇒ connector for battery holder
⇒ different items to be tested such as: wooden chopstick, small candle, metal fork, coins, pencil, plastic disposable pen, ice cube, glass of water, rubber eraser, cork, salt, drinking glass

WHAT TO DO

1. Copy the table with this project onto a piece of paper.

2. Place the batteries in the holder and attach the connector. Use a wire with an alligator clip to connect the positive end of the battery holder (red wire) to the positive end of the buzzer.

3. Attach the second wire with an alligator clip to the other end of the buzzer.

4. Connect the third wire with an alligator clip to the negative (black wire) end of the battery terminal.

5. You should have 2 empty clips on 2 unattached wire ends (Photo 1). Touch the clips on the ends of these wires together briefly to make sure that the buzzer will buzz. Then move the clips apart. Connect each of the different items to be tested between the empty clips, in turn (Photos 2 to 4). Record your observations in the chart.

6. For any trials of the items in which the buzzer didn't sound, try replacing the buzzer with the LED. Be sure that the long (positive) leg of the LED is attached to the positive wire from the battery.

7. Partially fill the glass with water, and attach it so that the metal of the clips is in the water. Note whether the buzzer can sound or not. Add some salt to the water and repeat the experiment.

TABLE

	buzzer on	buzzer off	LED on	LED off
wooden object				
fork				
candle				
ice cube				
glass				
coin				
pen				
water with salt				
water without salt				
dime				

WHAT HAPPENED

The buzzer worked when you tested the dime and fork and other metal things. Metals are conductors, substances that let electricity pass through them easily. When the wood, glass, and candle were connected to the circuit, the buzzer or light did not work, because electrons couldn't pass through them and the circuit wasn't complete; they are insulators or nonconductors. Conductors allow electrons to move easily through them; insulators hold their electrons more tightly. What about water and ice? Well, it depends. Water that has a high mineral content (hard water) is more likely to allow a current to pass through than water that is soft, because hard water contains dissolved

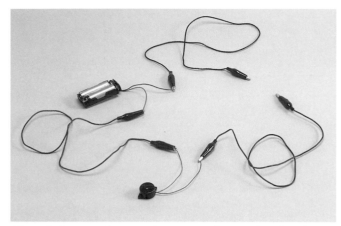

Photo 1. Setup with space between alligator clips for object to be tested.

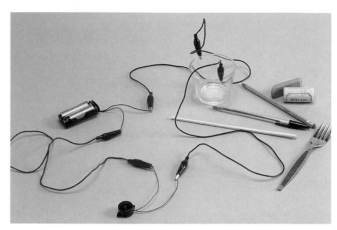

Photo 2. Circuit connected to a drinking glass.

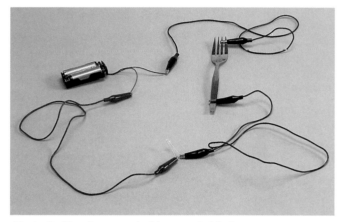

Photo 3. Circuit connected to a metal fork.

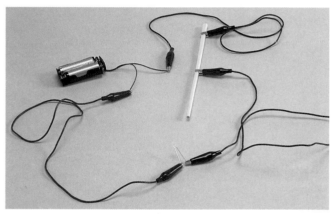

Photo 4. Circuit with a wooden chopstick.

mineral ions, which can carry a charge. Depending on what kind of water you have, the LED may have lit or not. When you added salt to the water, it formed ions. If there were enough ions, a current could pass through. An LED requires a much smaller current of electricity than a buzzer, so the LED may have lit when the buzzer didn't sound. To learn more about LEDs, see Led Astray.

CONVENTIONAL CURRENT

Early researchers of electricity didn't know that an electric current was caused by the passage of electrons. When they described the direction a current traveled through a wire, they said that the current went from the positive terminal of a battery through the wire to the negative terminal. However, they were wrong. We now know that electrons travel from the negative to the positive terminal. People still use the positive-to-negative idea when talking about circuits; we call this idea conventional current. The circuit diagrams in this book are drawn using the assumption of conventional current.

Going 'Round in Circuits

A closed circuit is an unbroken loop or path that an electrical current travels. It includes all components that the electrons travel through. One way to test to see if you have created a closed circuit is to make it work for you. You can't see the electrons moving, but you can see and sometimes hear the effects of this current on light bulbs or buzzers.

YOU WILL NEED

⇒ two 1-foot (30 cm) pieces of insulated bell wire
⇒ wire strippers
⇒ 1.5 to 3V light bulb and holder
⇒ AA battery
⇒ 1.5 to 3V electric buzzer
⇒ screw driver

WHAT TO DO

1. Use the wire strippers to remove a 1 inch (2.5 cm) piece of the plastic insulation from both ends of the pieces of insulated wire.

2. Screw the light bulb into the holder. Attach one end of the first wire to one terminal on the light bulb holder. (Depending on the type of holder, it may clip in place or you may have to turn a small screw to hold it in place.) Attach one end of the second wire to the other terminal on the bulb holder (Photo 1).

3. Place the free end of the first wire on a counter or tabletop and stand the battery on top of the wire so that it makes contact with the shiny metal bottom of the battery (negative terminal).

4. Touch the free end of the second wire to the positive terminal on the top of the battery (Photo 2). Watch to see if the light bulb lights. If it doesn't light up, check your connections. There should be a complete path or circuit from one terminal of the battery, through the wire, into the light bulb, through the second wire, and

back to the other terminal of the battery.

5. Try this project again, this time using a buzzer instead of the light bulb. Most buzzers will only work if they are connected to the correct terminals of the battery. If the buzzer doesn't make a sound, try switching the wires between the two terminals of the battery.

WHAT HAPPENED

When the wires were connected together to make a complete loop or circuit, the bulb or buzzer worked. The light bulb lit; the buzzer made a noise. The two terminals of the battery are of different materials. In this case, the outside of the battery is the negative terminal, which is zinc, and the positive terminal is carbon. When connected by the wire conductor and the electrolyte in the battery, there is a complete circuit. Electrons enter the wire from the terminal at the bottom of the battery. They travel into the light bulb or buzzer and cause the light to shine or the buzzer to sound. In a light bulb, the narrow

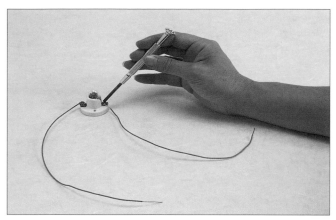

Photo 1. Attach the wires to the light bulb holder.

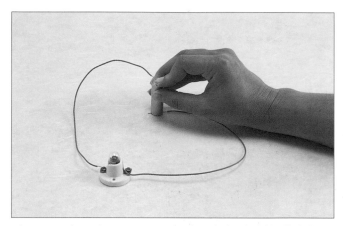

Photo 2. When the circuit is completed, the light bulb lights.

wire or filament gets so hot, because of the passing of electrons through a very thin wire, that it glows. The electrons move through the other wire beyond the bulb or buzzer and back to the terminal on the top of the battery. Within the battery, charged particles or ions moved from one terminal to the other to complete the circuit.

THOMAS ALVA EDISON

Every time you go to a movie, turn on a light bulb, or listen to the latest sound on a record player, you can thank Thomas Alva Edison for inventing or perfecting these things. Edison (1847–1931) was one of the greatest inventors who ever lived. During his life, he patented 1,093 different inventions, of which 365 were related to lighting and power.

Edison was unhappy at school and his mother had to teach him at home. By the age of 10 he began experimenting with chemistry and electricity. Soon he outgrew his space at home and by the age of 12 had created his own laboratory in the back of a train, where he worked selling newspapers and candy. Edison was the first to set up a commercial laboratory dedicated to research and development of new ideas. Most people associate Edison with the incandescent light bulb, which he perfected, but he invented the modern movie camera, created the carbon telephone transmitter, which extended the range of the telephone, and in 1882 opened the first commercial electric station on Pearl Street in Manhattan, New York City, the beginning of the U.S. lighting industry.

Bright Lights

Have you ever noticed that there are big lantern batteries that are 1.5 volt batteries and identical-looking ones that are 6 volts? Did you wonder what the difference was inside the battery? Are the chemicals different, or is it something else? Here is an experiment that will answer your questions. Warning: Do not ever try to cut into or open batteries.

YOU WILL NEED

⇒ 3 AA batteries

⇒ six 12-inch-long (30 cm) pieces of insulated copper wire

⇒ wire strippers

⇒ 1.5 to 3 V light bulb and holder

⇒ tape

WHAT TO DO

1. Using the wire strippers, remove about 1 inch (2.5 cm) of the plastic insulation from both ends of each of the pieces of insulated wire.

2. Attach one end of wire 1 to one terminal of the light bulb holder. Attach one end of wire 2 to the other light bulb holder terminal.

3. Tape the loose end of wire 1 to the positive terminal (top) of the first battery (Photo 1). Go to Step 4 for either series connection or parallel connection.

Series (Photo 2)

4. Tape one end of wire 3 to the negative terminal (bottom) of the first battery. Tape the other end of wire 3 to the positive terminal of battery 2.

5. Tape one end of wire 4 to the negative terminal of battery 2. Tape the other end of wire 4 to the positive terminal of battery 3.

6. Tape the unattached end of wire 2 to the negative terminal of battery 3 (see series diagram). Observe how brightly the light bulb shines. If the bulb doesn't light, check the

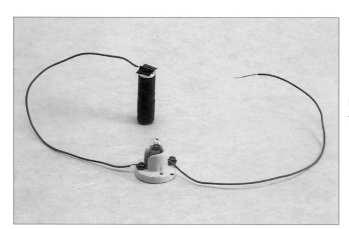

Photo 1. Beginning the connections.

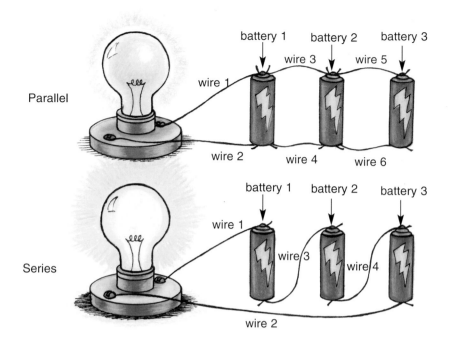

Parallel

Series

Diagram 1. Batteries connected in parallel and in series.

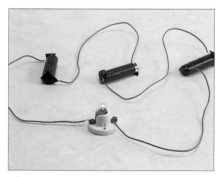

Photo 2. Series connection.

connections to see that they are all still attached. If that doesn't work, check the light bulb to see if it is burnt out, and check the batteries to see that they are still charged.

Parallel (Photo 3)

4. Tape one end of wire 3 to the positive terminal of the first battery next to wire 1. Tape the other end of wire 3 to the positive terminal of battery 2 (see parallel diagram).

5. Tape one end of wire 4 to the negative terminal of the

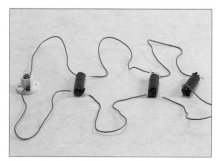

Photo 3. Parallel connection.

first battery and the other end of wire 4 to the negative terminal of battery 2.

6. Tape one end of wire 5 to the positive terminal of battery 2 and the other end to the positive terminal of battery 3.

7. Tape one end of the sixth piece of copper wire to the negative terminal of battery 2 and the other end to the negative terminal of battery 3.

8. Tape the unattached end of wire 2 to the negative terminal of battery 1. Observe how brightly the light bulb shines.

WHAT HAPPENED

When you connected the cells together in series, the light bulb glowed brightly. When the cells were connected in parallel, the bulb only glowed dimly. Each of the cells provides about 1.5 volts. When they are connected in series, the voltages add together to provide a 4.5 volt (1.5 × 3) supply. When connected in parallel, the voltage remains 1.5 volts.

Commercial batteries often are made of 4 cells joined together in parallel; this gives a longer-lasting 1.5 V battery. Batteries made from the same 4 cells connected in series provide a 6 V power supply.

Potato Polarity

You can't use a potato as a compass to find the magnetic north pole, but can you use it for a chemistry experiment? Let's find out.

YOU WILL NEED

⇒ large, fresh raw potato
⇒ knife
⇒ two 4-inch (10 cm) pieces of insulated copper wire
⇒ wire strippers
⇒ 2 insulated wires with alligator clips at each end
⇒ 9-volt battery

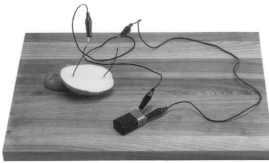

Photo 1. Potato wired to battery.

WHAT TO DO

1. Cut the potato in half.

2. Use the wire strippers to remove about 1 inch (2.5 cm) of the plastic insulation from both ends of the pieces of wire without the alligator clips.

3. Using the wires with alligator clips, attach one of the wires to the positive terminal of the battery and the other wire to the negative terminal of the battery.

4. Firmly embed the loose ends of the wires without clips in the

Photo 2. Closeup of potato, showing the green color at positive end and bubbles at negative end of wire.

potato. Make sure there is at least 1 inch (2.5 cm) distance between the two wires (Photo 1).

5. Clip the unattached end of the wire from the positive terminal of the battery to a potato wire. Clip the loose end of the wire from the negative terminal of the battery to the second potato wire. Observe what happens.

WHAT HAPPENED

After a minute or two, you saw something green coming from the wire attached to the positive terminal and bubbles coming from the wire attached to the negative terminal. The current flow caused a chemical reaction. The green color around the positive electrode occurs because the copper in the wire is losing electrons and changing into copper ions. Copper ions have a bluish green color, and they dissolve in the liquid of the potato. The bubbles at the negative electrode are hydrogen gas, formed when electrons go into the water of the potato, causing the water to split apart, releasing hydrogen.

It's Done with Magnets

Electricity and magnetism are closely related to each other. People had long suspected this relationship, and had noticed that pieces of metal were magnetized by strokes of lightning. Understanding of the connection between magnetism and electricity began quite by accident. In the years following Volta's invention of the battery, scientists all over Europe began to experiment with electricity. A Danish scientist named Hans Christian Oersted (1777–1851) made an important discovery. During a lecture on electricity in 1819, Oersted was demonstrating the voltaic pile, an early version of the battery, when he noticed something unusual. When he connected the wires of the voltaic pile so that current was flowing, the needle of a nearby compass turned. Oersted guessed that an electric current must cause a magnetic field around the wire it was flowing through, and that the field must be strong

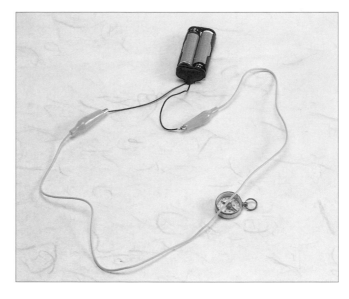

Photo 1. Oersted's experiment: a compass placed near a current-carrying wire.

enough to turn the compass's north-seeking arrow away from the direction it normally would point because of the earth's magnetic field.

French scientist André Marie Ampère (1775–1836), after hearing of Oersted's discovery, began to perform experiments with batteries and wires. He discovered that a current traveling through a wire causes a cylinder of magnetic attraction, or magnetic field, to form around the wire. He also dis-

covered that the magnetic field increases when the current through the wire increases, and decreases as you go further away from the wire, and that when parallel wires carry current, their fields affect each other. Ampère discovered that coiling the wire intensified the magnetic field. The coil of wire through which a current can flow is called a solenoid. The solenoid is a basic ingredient of electromagnets, motors, and generators, as we shall see.

Circuit Seekers

Sometimes a circuit may have an electrical current, but it may not be strong enough to turn on a light or operate a buzzer. How can you measure this current, if you can't see it? An instrument called a galvanometer can detect and measure small electric currents, so we will make one now.

WHAT TO DO

1. Use scissors or a craft knife to make two ½-inch (1 cm) cuts about half an inch apart in the middle of two opposite sides of the cardboard (see Photo 1).

Photo 1. Cardboard bent into position with first turn of wire wrapped around compass.

2. Place the compass in the middle of the piece of cardboard. Bend the ½ inch (1 cm) strips of the cardboard up, so they form a holder.

3. Wrap the wire around the compass and holder, leaving about 6 inches (15 cm) of wire at both ends. This is your galvanometer (Photo 2).

Photo 2. Wire wound around compass.

4. Twist the ends of the wire, so that the wire does not unravel from the galvanometer. Look at the compass needle and observe how it is pointing.

5. Attach the free ends of the galvanometer wire to the circuit; for example, to the battery terminals. Look at the compass needle when the wires are attached.

WHAT HAPPENED

Wrapping the wire around the compass created a galvanometer. When a current ran

YOU WILL NEED

⇒ 12 yards (11 m) of very fine lacquered or varnished bell wire
⇒ square piece of cardboard 1 inch (2.5 cm) larger than the diameter of the compass
⇒ compass
⇒ source of current, such as one AA battery and battery holder, or lemon setup from Lemon Lights
⇒ scissors or craft knife

through the coil, the needle moved. A magnetic field perpendicular to the wires was produced around the coil of wire. A compass needle is a small suspended magnet. A suspended magnet will normally align north–south because of the Earth's magnetic field. If the magnetic field inside the coil was in a different direction from the magnetic field of the Earth, the needle turned away from the Earth's magnetic field when the current was flowing. A magnetic field can be seen in a straight wire connected to a power source also, but coiling the wire created a stronger field, allowing you to detect even very small currents.

RIGHT-HAND RULE

You can always remember the direction in which the magnetic field travels around the wire if you use your right hand. Place your hand so that the thumb of your right hand points along the wire in the direction of the conventional current flow (from the positive terminal to the negative terminal). The magnetic field around the wire moves in the same direction as your fingers curl around the wire. This is called the right-hand rule. The north-seeking needle of a compass placed anywhere on your hand in the wire's magnetic field will point along your hand towards your fingers.

It was Michael Faraday who introduced the idea of magnetic lines of force. These are the lines of force you see if you sprinkle iron filings near a magnet. The iron filings are an indication of the magnet's field.

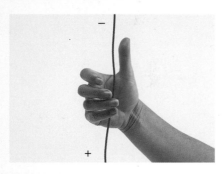

Conventional current travels from positive (at the bottom of the picture) to negative (at the top of the picture).

Where's the Magnet?

Grab a bar magnet. It probably has an N, for north-seeking end, on one side and an S, for south, on the other side. Now find a long iron nail. Does it have a north and south pole? Let's see.

YOU WILL NEED

⇒ long iron nail

⇒ 3 feet (90 cm) of insulated wire

⇒ holder for 2 AA batteries

⇒ 2 AA batteries

⇒ snap connector for battery holder

⇒ wire strippers

⇒ small metallic objects of iron, steel, or nickel that can be attracted to a magnet; for example, iron or steel paper clips

WHAT TO DO

1. Have an adult strip the ends of the wire off to expose 1 inch (2.5 cm) of bare wire.

2. Leave about 8 inches (20 cm) of loose wire at the end; then, starting at the point of the nail, tightly wrap the wire around the nail. There is a trick to wrapping the wire around the nail so that it doesn't unravel as fast as you wind it. On the first twist, loop the short end of the wire under the wire and pull it into a knot (see Photo 1). In this way, it will stay put while you are winding the rest of the wire. When you have

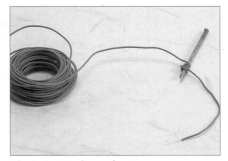

Photo 1. Winding of wire.

reached the end of the nail, loop the end into a knot around the nail also.

3. Place the batteries in the battery holder. Attach the bare ends of the wire wrapped around the nail to the terminals of the battery holder.

4. When you have made the connection, try attracting small metal objects with the end of the nail (Photo 2).

5. Disconnect one end wire from the battery and try to pick up the metallic objects.

Warning: Be careful to disconnect the battery after a few seconds, because the amount of current going through the wire is quite large and it could cause the wire to heat up. Do not use the magnet near computer equipment, software, or watches.

WHAT HAPPENED

You made an electromagnet. When an electrical current passes through a wire, a magnetic field forms around it. When the battery was connected to the coil of wire surrounding the nail, you were able to pick up small objects made of iron,

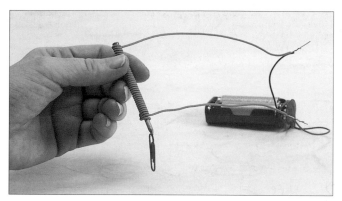

Photo 2. Wrapped nail, connected to battery, attracts a paper clip.

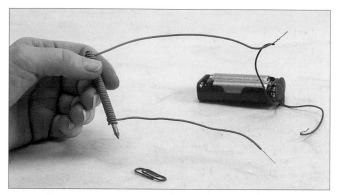

Photo 3. When the coil is disconnected from the battery, the paper clip is not attracted.

nickel, cobalt or steel with the nail. Using a magnetic metal (in this case, the iron nail) as the core of the coil increases the strength of the magnet. You can increase the strength of your electromagnet further by increasing the number of coils around the nail, or by increasing the voltage of the battery you use, but don't use anything larger than a 6-volt lantern battery for safety reasons. When you disconnected the battery from the coil of wire, the magnetic field was gone, and the metal objects were no longer attracted to the nail. The magnetic field of an electromagnet with a metal core can be hundreds or thousands of times stronger than the wire coil alone. Electromagnets are used in many devices such as motors, generators, doorbells, telephone headsets and electric meters.

Motor City

Detroit is sometimes called Motor City, because it is where the automotive industry began and so many automobiles were manufactured there. But what is a motor, anyway? This experiment will give you an idea how a simple motor works.

YOU WILL NEED

⇒ plastic cup

⇒ 2 large uncoated wire paper clips

⇒ 6-volt lantern battery

⇒ masking or electrical tape

⇒ small disc-shaped magnet

⇒ 39 inches (1 m) of fine coated copper wire (about 20 gauge)

⇒ bottle of nail polish about 1 inch (2.5 cm) in diameter

⇒ 2 wires with alligator clips on each end

⇒ wire strippers or a craft knife

WHAT TO DO

1. Straighten the outer end of each paper clip so it forms a long straight section, but leave a loop on the other end (see Photo 1).

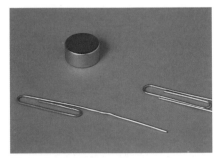
Photo 1. Straightened paper clip, magnet, and normal paper clip.

2. Invert the cup, and tape the straightened end of each paper clip onto one end of the diameter of the bottom of the cup, so that the bottom of the loop is about 1 inch (2.5 cm) above the surface of the cup (Photo 2).

Photo 2. Paper clips taped to cup, with magnet in place.

3. Have an adult use wire strippers or a craft knife to remove the insulating coating from about 1 inch (2.5 cm) at one end of the 39-inch copper wire. Leaving the stripped end sticking out, wrap the wire, always in the same direction, around a nail polish bottle 6 to 10 times to make a coil; remove from bottle. Let the coated end of the wire stick out on the diameter directly opposite the uncoated end of the wire. Carefully wrap the coil with two or three strips of tape to keep it a tight compact unit, or wrap the wire around itself to hold it (Photo 3).

4. Have an adult use a craft knife to scrape the coating off about 1 inch (2.5 cm) of one side of the coated end of the wire only. If all of the coating comes off, paint one side with nail polish and allow it to dry before continuing.

5. Place the magnet in the center of the upended bottom of the plastic cup, between the paper clips.

6. Hang the coil on the paper clips so that it is suspended by the two ends of the wire in the clip loops. You will have to adjust the ends of the wire and the paper clips so that the coil can turn freely between the two paper clips (Photo 3). This is the most difficult part, and it may take several tries to have the coil spinning evenly.

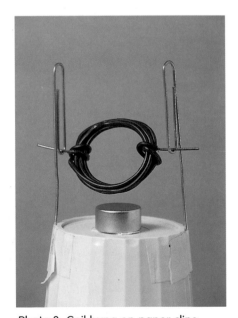
Photo 3. Coil hung on paper clips.

7. Once the coil is mounted correctly, attach one end of a wire with an alligator clip to the positive terminal of the battery. Attach one end of the second wire with an alligator clip to the negative terminal of the battery. Then connect the free end of each wire to the straight part of one of the paper clips, below the loops (Photo 4). Give the coil a gentle push and watch it spin.

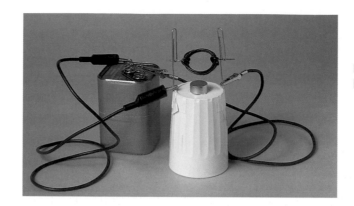

Photo 4. Setup with battery connected.

WHAT HAPPENED

You have made a very simple kind of electric motor. When you connected the battery to the paper clips, you completed a circuit from the battery, through one paper clip, into the coil, through the other paper clip, and back to the battery. When current flowed through the wire coil, the coil acted like an electromagnet, because when electricity flows through a wire, it creates a magnetic field around it. The magnetic field created a twisting force on the coil, which pushed one side of the coil towards the magnet on the cup, and one side away, which caused the coil to turn. Then, when the coil turned, the painted or coated part of the wire touched the paper clip. No current could flow through the coating, which broke the circuit. The current stopped, but the lightweight wire coil kept spinning, because the force of its own moving weight carried the coil forward until the bare section of wire touched the paper clip again, completing the circuit again. The electric field changed when the current was broken. This caused the coil to keep turning.

MOTORS

Motors are devices that change other forms of energy, such as electrical energy or the chemical energy in gasoline, into mechanical energy or motion. The type of electric motor you will use in the other experiments in this book is called a DC motor. DC stands for direct current, which is the type of electric current produced by batteries. In a direct current circuit, electric current travels through a circuit in one direction only. A DC motor has coils of wire with a metal core, which makes up the rotor, or armature. The rotor turns between two stationary (unmoving) magnets. When the moving coil cuts the lines of force of the stationary magnet, rotational force is produced, which rotates the coil of the electromagnet. The ends of the wire from the coil move back and forth between two contacts, or brushes, as the rotor turns. Each time there is a connection to a different one of the contacts, the direction of the current changes. The electromagnet is alternately attracted to or repelled by the poles of the permanent magnet in the motor, which causes the rotor to spin. Motors are everywhere, from the one in your electric blender to the one that starts your car.

MICHAEL FARADAY AND INDUCTION

English scientist Michael Faraday (1791–1867) built the world's first electric motor. In 1821, after hearing of the discoveries of Oersted and Ampère, Faraday built a motor in which a magnet would rotate about a conductor carrying a current. He was interested in the possibility of converting magnetism into electricity. In 1831, he worked with a welded iron ring 6 inches (15 cm) in diameter. He wrapped a coil of wire around one side of the ring and another coil around the opposite side. The coils were not connected. He connected a galvanometer to one coil. When he connected the second coil to a battery, the galvanometer needle moved, and when he disconnected it, the needle moved also. A current flowing in one coil was momentarily induced in the other coil. Faraday had discovered electromagnetic induction (see Human Dynamo). This was an extremely important discovery, because it served as the basis for many electricity-producing machines including motors and generators.

Human Dynamo

In 1831, Michael Faraday built the first electric generator. He had a copper disk suspended in between the poles of a strong magnet. The device was connected to a galvanometer. When he turned the disk with a crank, the galvanometer needle moved, indicating that a current was flowing. A generator is a machine that converts mechanical energy into electrical energy. Faraday's generator produced DC or direct current, and is called a dynamo. This is another example of electromagnetic induction at work.

In 1873, an exhibition that showcased the modern devices of the day was held in Vienna, Austria. At this exhibition a workman accidentally discovered that a dynamo was a DC motor working in reverse. By mistake he connected two dynamos together incorrectly and the second one began to spin on its own, like a motor. Here is another way to turn a DC motor into a dynamo or generator.

YOU WILL NEED

⇒ 1.5 to 3 V DC motor

⇒ galvanometer from Circuit Detective

⇒ 2 wires with alligator clips on both ends

WHAT TO DO

1. Attach one wire with an alligator clip to one end of the galvanometer wire. Clip a second wire with an alligator clip to the second end of the galvanometer wire. Attach the free ends of the wires that have alligator clips to the prongs of the motor (Photo 1).

2. Use your fingers to spin the shaft at the other end of the motor (Photo 2). Watch the needle on the galvanometer as you do this.

WHAT HAPPENED

Usually a motor converts electrical or chemical energy into mechanical energy, but we reversed things by turning the motor by hand. When you turned the shaft of the motor, you were causing the coil of wire inside the motor to turn around. When a coil of wire turns around a magnet, or when a magnet is pushed very quickly through a coil of wire, there is an electric current pro-

Photo 1. Motor attached to galvanometer.

Photo 2. Motor with knob being turned.

duced in the wire. You turned the motor into a generator and produced a small electric current. This caused the compass needle inside your galvanome-

ter to change direction as the current passed through the coil of wire, creating a magnetic field.

Transformers: More Than Meets the Eye

In Circuit Seekers, you created a galvanometer, which detected current. In this experiment you can use this device to learn about electromagnetic induction.

YOU WILL NEED

⇒ electromagnet from Where's the Magnet?

⇒ galvanometer from Circuit Seekers
⇒ long iron nail
⇒ 4 to 5 feet (1.2 to 1.5 m) of insulated wire
⇒ battery holder for 2 AA batteries
⇒ 2 AA batteries
⇒ wire strippers

WHAT TO DO

1. Have an adult use the wire strippers to remove 1 inch (2.5 cm) of plastic insulation from both ends of the wire.

2. Leave about 18 inches (45 cm) of wire unwound and, starting ½ inch (1 cm) above the point of the nail, tightly wrap the wire around the nail the same way you did in Where's the Magnet. When you reach the head of the nail, tie a knot in the end of the wire and make sure that there is about 18 inches (45 cm) of wire unwound on this end as well (Photo 1).

Photo 1. Wire wrapped around nail.

3. Attach the ends of the wire wrapped around the nail to the wires from the galvanometer (Photo 2).

4. Place the electromagnet from Where's the Magnet close to the wired nail attached to the galvanometer, but detach one wire from the battery. Move the galvanometer as far away as possible from the electromagnet.

5. Connect the electromagnet to the battery (Photo 3); then disconnect one wire (Photo 4). Repeat. Watch what happens to the needle of the galvanometer as you disconnect and reconnect the wire.

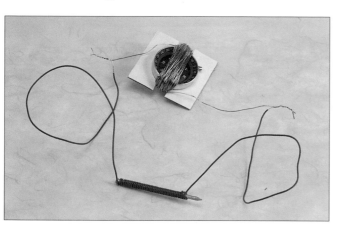

Photo 2. Galvanometer attached to wire wrapped around nail.

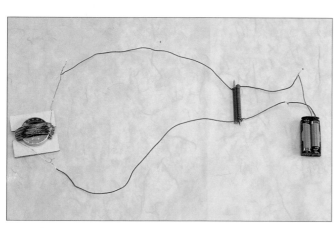

Photo 3. Galvanometer with electromagnet connected.

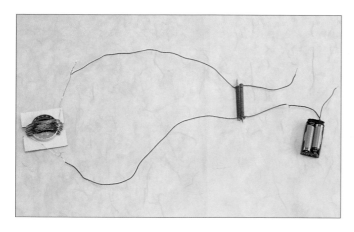

Photo 4. Galvanometer with electromagnet disconnected.

WHAT HAPPENED

When you close or open the circuit through the electromagnet (the green-wire-wrapped nail in the photo), the compass needle in the galvanometer moves. When the current flowing through the circuit is constant, the needle returns to its original location. When you close or open the circuit, you change the direction of the electrical field around the electromagnet. The moving magnetic field of the electromagnet causes an electric current to be produced in the nearby coil of wire around the nail in the galvanometer circuit, even though it wasn't touching the electromagnet. This is an example of electromagnetic induction. (If you hold the electromagnet too close to the galvanometer, the compass needle is attracted to the magnet, so you must be careful to keep them far enough apart.)

TRANSFORMERS

When electrical energy is transmitted over large distances, a lot of energy can be lost in the form of heat. The amount of heat produced in the power lines is related to the amount of current that travels in the lines. The current traveling in power lines changes direction 50 or 60 times a minute. This type of current is called AC or alternating current. In order to reduce the amount of heat loss, power companies use transformers to change the electric energy so that it has a lower current but a very high voltage.

Transformers make use of electromagnetic induction. The current travels through a wire to the transformer. The transformer has 2 sets of coils, wrapped around an iron core. The two sets of coils aren't touching each other. To step up the current to higher voltage, the incoming (input) current goes to a primary coil around the core. This coil has fewer turns of wire around the core than the secondary (output) coil. The alternating current makes a magnetic field that continually changes direction. The iron core transfers this field to the secondary coil, where it induces an output current in the secondary coil. The output current has higher voltage if there are more turns in the secondary coil wrapped around the core than in the primary coil. High voltage power lines carry electricity which is 220,000 V to 500,000 V. When the current gets near your house, it passes through several step-down transformers that lower the voltage. The electricity you use in your home is 110 or 220 V, depending on where you live.

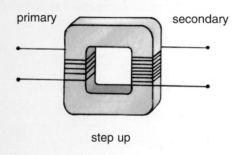

step up

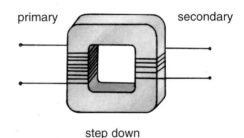

step down

Step-up (left) and step-down (right) transformers.

Circuit Rider

To turn on an electrical device like a light or buzzer, you need to make a complete electric circuit. The simplest circuits include only a power supply (like a battery), a single device (like a light bulb), and the wires to connect them together. More complicated circuits can contain several batteries linked together, a number of different devices such as switches, transistors, capacitors, LEDs, and resistors. This section introduces some of these devices.

SIGN LANGUAGE: ELECTRIC SYMBOLS

There are many different kinds of signs and symbols that you see every day. You'll immediately recognize a stop sign or the sign for a curve in the road. Electricity has its own symbols, too. No matter where you go in the world, these electrical symbols mean the same thing. People use them as a form of shorthand to draw an electrical circuit. Later in the book, you will learn how to read circuits drawn with these symbols, when you make circuits with your own electronic board.

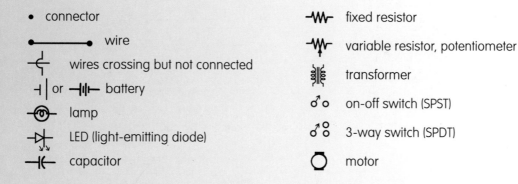

- connector
- wire
- wires crossing but not connected
- battery
- lamp
- LED (light-emitting diode)
- capacitor

- fixed resistor
- variable resistor, potentiometer
- transformer
- on-off switch (SPST)
- 3-way switch (SPDT)
- motor

Resistance Is Futile

In this project, we will use commercial resistors, components designed to control the amount of voltage and current flowing through a circuit. Take a close look at a resistor. It looks like a tiny cylinder with colored bands around it. The colored stripes on a resistor tell the user the resistance of the component in ohms. Since resistors are so tiny, it is easier to read the colored stripes than it would be to read tiny numerals. Here's how to tell the value of a resistor.

RESISTANCE

Resistance is anything that opposes the flow of electricity in a circuit. Everything in a circuit causes some resistance, even the wire. However, some things have more resistance than others. Some electrical components, such as the filament in a light bulb, are designed to have high resistance. When the electrons flow through the very narrow wire of a light bulb, it begins to glow and give off energy as light. Sometimes resistance results in the resistor heating up, as does the heating element on your toaster or stove. The unit used to measure the amount of resistance is the ohm, abbreviated by the greek letter omega, Ω, named after Georg Simon Ohm (1787–1854), a German scientist. He studied the amount of current and voltage flowing through various conductors and discovered the mathematical relationship between them (see Ohm's Law), which he published in 1827.

YOU WILL NEED

⇒ 5 resistors of different value
⇒ pencil
⇒ paper
⇒ resistor stripe chart (p.58)

WHAT TO DO

1. Turn the resistor so that the gold or silver band is on your right.

2. Look up the first stripe of color on the left side of the resistor in the chart and write

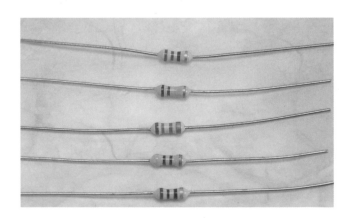

Photo 1. Resistors. The stripes indicate amounts of resistance.

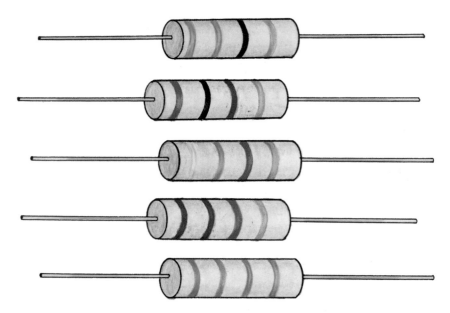

Diagram 1. Samples of resistors. Look at the 5 resistors pictured and consult the chart to determine the value of each. (Answers are upside down on page 58).

Georg Simon Ohm tested a number of different conductors. He discovered that when he increased the voltage in a circuit, if the conductor stayed the same, there was a constant increase in the current in the circuit. This was because the conductor had a certain resistance that didn't vary. He found that the voltage (V) of a circuit was equal to the current (I) multiplied by the resistance (R) of a circuit: $V = I \times R$. This formula will help you figure out whether or not a particular circuit is going to work, or why it doesn't. When you use a battery of a certain voltage to supply electricity to a circuit, increasing the resistance decreases the current. Decreasing the resistance increases the current. Too much current can heat up the wires and wear out the battery quickly. Too little current means that electrical devices such as light bulbs and buzzers will not work. Not all resistors obey Ohm's Law, but commercial resistors do, and so do most metals.

down the corresponding number from column 1. This is the first number of your resistor.

3. Look up the second stripe of color from the left side in the 2nd stripe column of the chart and write down the corresponding number. This is the second number of your resistor.

4. Locate the third colored band from the left on your resistor, and look up the value in the 3rd stripe column of the chart. In the 3rd stripe column, the color has a different value than in the 1st and 2nd stripe columns. It is a multiple of 10. Write down the number to the right of the two you already have.

5. The first two numbers are the first two digits of the resistance. For example, 33 represents thirty-three. Multiply this number by the 3rd stripe column number. You won't need a calculator. Just add the appropriate number of zeros to the right of the two-digit number. For example, if your 3rd stripe column number is × 100 (representing "times 100"), just add two zeros to the right of 33 to multiply it by 100, for 3300 ohms.

6. The fourth colored stripe from the left tells you how accurate the value of the resistor is. This value is called the tolerance of the resistor. It is expressed as a percentage of the resistance.

RESISTOR STRIPE COLORS AND THEIR VALUES

color	1st stripe	2nd stripe	3rd stripe	4th stripe
black	0	0	×1	
brown	1	1	×10	
red	2	2	×100	
orange	3	3	×1 000	
yellow	4	4	×10 000	
green	5	5	×100 000	
blue	6	6	×1 000 000	
violet	7	7		
gray	8	8		
white	9	9		
gold				5%
silver				10%
no color				20%

One way to remember the order of the colors is to use the first letter of each color for the first letter of a word in a silly sentence. The letters in order are: BBROYGBVGW. We use this: Black Bugs Raid Our Young Garden, But Violets Grow Wild. See if you can make up sentences of your own to remember them!

Answers: From top to bottom: 33 ohms, 1000 ohms, 450 ohms, 220 ohms, 65 000 ohms.

LED Astray

Let's look at a light-emitting diode, or LED. It's possible you may find one in your home; otherwise buy some at an electrical supply store. If you look closely, you can see that one wire leg of the LED is slightly longer than the other. The longer side is the positive side (+) of the LED; the shorter side is negative (Photo 1). LEDs come in many colors besides red (Photo 2). You can find them in yellow, green, orange and sometimes blue. These tiny colored lights are used in portable disc players, toys, and even on your computer. Do not confuse LED with LCD, which stands for liquid crystal display, like the one found on a calculator.

YOU WILL NEED

⇒ 3 wires with alligator clips at each end
⇒ LED (light-emitting diode)
⇒ resistor (about 100 ohms)
⇒ holder for 2 AA batteries
⇒ 2 AA batteries
⇒ battery connector

WHAT TO DO

1. Put the batteries in the battery holder and attach the battery connector. The red or colored wire usually comes from the battery holder's positive (+) terminal.

Photo 1. LED. Positive terminal is longer wire.

2 Attach wire #1 with an alligator clip to the positive wire from the battery connector. Attach wire #2 with an alligator clip to the negative wire from the connector.

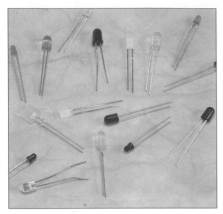

Photo 2. LEDs of different colors and sizes.

3. Clip the second end of wire #1 to the positive leg (long end) of the LED.

4. Clip the loose end of the wire attached to the negative terminal of the battery (wire #2) to one end of the resistor. Attach the third wire (wire #3) with an alligator clip to the loose end of the resistor, and connect the free end of wire #3 to the negative side of the LED. You should have a complete circuit (Photo 3).

5. If the light did not turn on, check all the connections to make sure you have the positive and negative sides in the right place!

WHAT HAPPENED

The LED lit up when connected in a complete circuit. Diodes will only allow the current to travel through them in one direction, which is why you needed to connect the positive end of the battery to the positive end of the LED. Many devices and appliances use LEDs. They don't take up as much room as a regular light bulb, so it is easier to use them in small spaces. They are very sturdy and don't break easily when dropped. Compared to a small light bulb, an LED lasts a very long time before burning out. The big advantage LEDs have is that they don't need as large a current as a light bulb,

so devices with LEDs that are battery-operated don't run down as quickly as they would with light bulbs. Because LEDs don't need much current, it is important to reduce the number of amperes in the circuit with a resistor so that the LED doesn't burn out (see Resistance Is Futile).

DIODES

"Diode" stands for "2 electrodes." A diode is an electrical component that allows current to flow through it in one direction only. The diodes we use today are made of silicon, a semiconductor*, with some impurities added to it at each end. The diode has two layers—one that attracts electrons and one that gives up electrons easily. When the current flows, the electrons pass from one layer to the other to complete the circuit.

A light-emitting diode (LED) has some special elements added to the silicon of the diode that cause light to be emitted when current passes through it from the positive to the negative direction. The light output of an LED increases when the current increases.

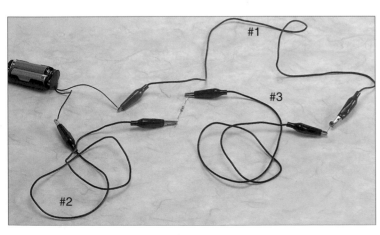

Photo 3. LED and resistor in a circuit.

Experiments with Your Own Electronic Board

Now that you have learned about circuits, LEDs, resistors, and batteries, it's time to put that knowledge to some use. Look closely at Photo 1 (p. 62). The white plastic board you see is called a breadboard or a socket board. Below the holes, inside the board, are metal strips (see Diagram 1). The strips run in rows in a left-right direction (blue lines on diagram).

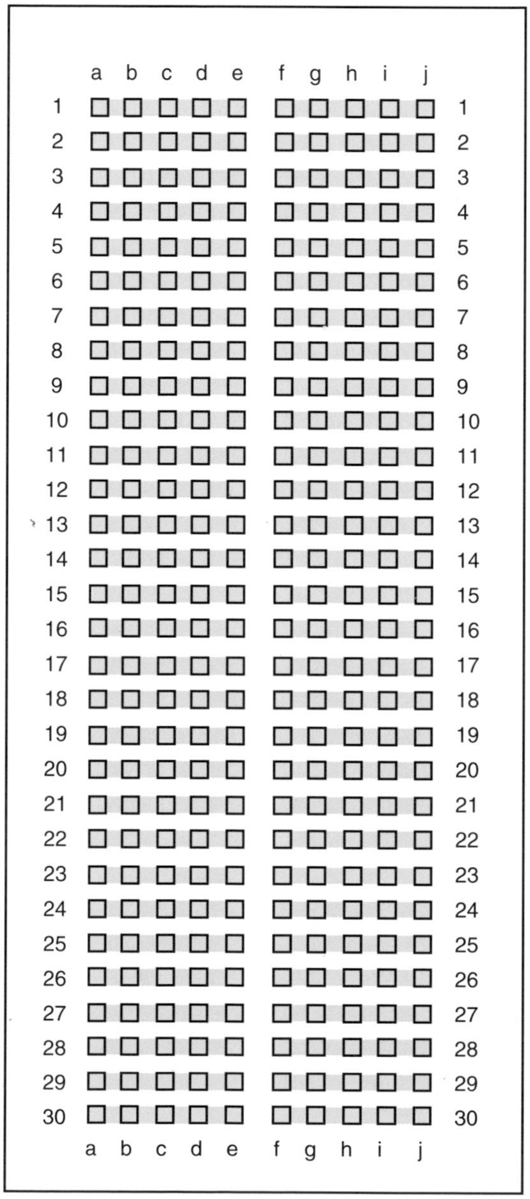

In this section of the book, each project includes a circuit diagram, called a schematic. Follow it to make your circuit. Refer to the symbols chart on page 55 so you can tell what the symbols in the schematic mean. To use the board, build a circuit by inserting the electrical components (parts that make up the circuit) into the correct holes. When the ends of the components' wires touch a metal strip, they connect and make a circuit. When you correctly attach your components, you can make buzzers buzz,

Diagram 1. Diagram of breadboard. Blue lines indicate metal strips that conduct electricity.

Photo 1. Empty board with jump wires.

in the breadboard. Not a problem! You can either twist the ends of jump wires (small insulated connecting wires) into the holes in the prongs of the components, or you can use thin, insulated wires with the ends stripped to expose the copper wire inside. Wrap one end of the stripped wire around the component prong and put the other end of the stripped wire in the hole in the breadboard.

lights light, and resistors resist.

Putting the components into the breadboard is like solving a simple puzzle. All you have to do is match the components to the correct letters and numbers given in the project; then stick the wires into the holes. Use the photos for reference.

Note: Some of the components may not fit into the holes

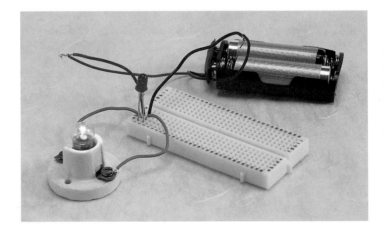

Photo 2. Breadboard with things connected from one of the experiments.

Get Serious

⇒ breadboard

⇒ 2 LEDs (light-emitting diodes)

⇒ holder for 2 AA batteries

⇒ 2 AA batteries

⇒ battery connector

WHAT TO DO

Series Circuit

1. Push the positive terminal (longer leg) of one LED into a1, and push the negative terminal (shorter leg) of the same LED into a2. On the schematics, the flat end of the LED triangle indicates the positive terminal; the pointy end of the triangle is the negative terminal (see Diagram 2).

Imagine this: You have a 10-foot (3 m) string of tiny light bulbs all connected to each other. One of the light bulbs burns out. What happens? That depends on how the light bulbs are connected together in the string of lights. If they are connected in series, so that the current must run through each of the bulbs in turn, all the lights will go out and you will have to test each and every one of the bulbs to see which one is no longer working. If you had a string of lights that were connect- ed in parallel, so that the current *runs through each bulb separately, all the lights would still be on, except for the one that burned out. Here's how it works using your breadboard. (See page 55 for electrical symbol chart, if neces- sary, and use schematic diagrams for reference to assemble your cir- cuit.)*

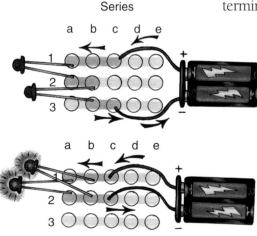

Series

Parallel

Diagram 1. Setup for series and parallel cir- cuits, showing current flow.

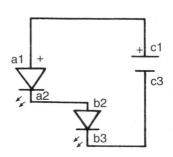

Diagram 2. Schematic of series circuit.

2. Push the positive terminal of the second LED into b2, and push the negative terminal of the same LED into b3.

3. Push the positive (+) battery wire into c1, and push the negative battery wire (-) into c3 (Photo 1). Will the LEDs light?

Photo 1. Series circuit.

Parallel Circuit

1. Push the positive terminal of one LED into a1, and push the negative terminal of the same LED into a2.

2. Push the positive terminal of the second LED into b1, and push the negative terminal of the same LED into hole b2.

3. Push the positive battery wire into c1 and the negative battery wire into c2 (Photo 2). Will the LEDs light?

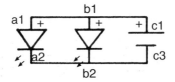

Diagram 3. Schematic of parallel circuit.

WHAT HAPPENED

The LEDs did not light up in the series setup, but did light up in the parallel setup. When the LEDs are connected in series, the circuit has more resistance than when they are connected in parallel, because the resistance of the 2 LEDs is added together. The current traveling through the LEDs in series is much less than the current in the parallel circuit. Remember earlier when we talked about resistance, and said $V = I \times R$ (voltage = current times resistance)? If the

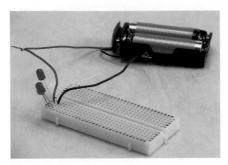

Photo 2. Parallel circuit.

resistance of a circuit increases, the current decreases. In the series circuit, the current is too small to allow the LEDs to light up. In the parallel circuit, if you increase the number of LEDs, you increase the amount of current flowing through the system. The total resistance decreases, so the total current increases compared to a circuit with a single LED or the LEDs in series. In the parallel circuit, each LED has its own path, and each of the LEDs will light. The lights in your house are connected in parallel. If one light burns out, the others will stay on. (However, if you put too many light bulbs or other electrical devices on the same circuit in your house, you will increase the current to a level where you will blow a fuse or trip a circuit breaker.)

Standing in Your Shadow

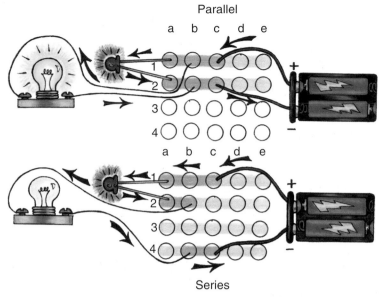

Diagram 1. Series and parallel setup, showing current flow.

You learned about series and parallel circuits in Get Serious, but can you always predict that your lights will or won't light? Explain this one.

YOU WILL NEED

⇒ LED (light-emitting diode)
⇒ miniature light bulb (1.5 to 3 V) and holder with connecting wires
⇒ holder for 2 AA batteries
⇒ 2 AA batteries
⇒ battery connector

WHAT TO DO

1. Push the positive terminal of one LED into a1, and the negative terminal of the same LED into hole a2.

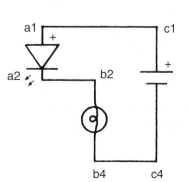

Diagram 2. Schematic of series circuit, Steps 1 to 3.

2. Push one wire of the light bulb holder into b2, and the other wire of the light bulb holder into hole b4.

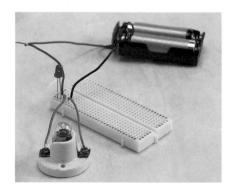

Photo 1. Setup for series.

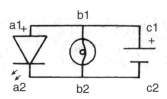

Diagram 3. Schematic of parallel circuit.

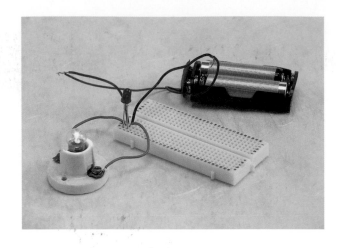

Photo 2. Setup for parallel.

3. Push the positive battery wire into hole c1 and the negative battery wire into hole c4. What happens? (Diagram 2).

4. Leave the LED attached as in Step 1 and move the wire of the light bulb holder from b4 to b1.

5. Move the negative wire of the battery holder from c4 to c2 (Diagram 3). Now what happens?

WHAT HAPPENED

In Step 3, when the battery was connected, the LED went on, but the light bulb didn't. In Step 5, both lights went on. When you connected the light bulb and the LED together in series, the current went through both the LED and the light bulb (Step 3). This increased the circuit's resistance and, as when two LEDs were connected in series (in Get Serious), there wasn't enough current to allow both the light bulb and the LED to light. There was enough current for the LED alone to light (Photo 1). This is because the light bulb has a lower resistance than a second LED would have had (see page 63). The total resistance in the circuit is lower than with 2 LEDs, so the current is still large enough to light the LED. When the LED and light bulb are connected in parallel in Step 5, there is less total resistance than in the series circuit; the amount of current traveling through the circuit increases, and there is enough current through the LED and the light bulb to cause them both to light (Photo 2).

Resistance to Change

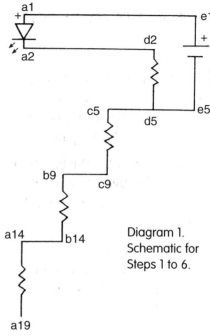

Diagram 1. Schematic for Steps 1 to 6.

You have seen the difference that changing the resistance can make to your circuit. But what do you think would happen if you had several resistors in a circuit? Here is a way to tell!

YOU WILL NEED

⇒ breadboard
⇒ LED (light-emitting diode)
⇒ Four 1000-ohm resistors (stripes: brown, black, red, gold)
⇒ holder for two AA batteries
⇒ Two AA batteries
⇒ battery connector

WHAT TO DO

1. Push the positive terminal of the LED into a1 on the breadboard, and the negative terminal of the LED into a2. (See Diagram 1 for Steps 1 to 6.)

2. Push one wire of the first resistor into d2, and the other wire of the same resistor into d5.

3. Push one end of the next resistor into c5 and the other end into c9.

4. Push one end of another resistor into b9 and the other end into b14.

5. Place the final resistor with one end in a14 and the other end in a19.

6. Connect the battery so that the wire connected to the positive terminal is in e1 and the

Photo 1. Circuit setup with all four resistors in series, showing the connection with a single LED.

wire connected to the negative terminal is in e5. Observe the LED.

7. Carefully disconnect the negative wire of the battery holder and push it into hole e9 (Diagram 2); observe the LED.

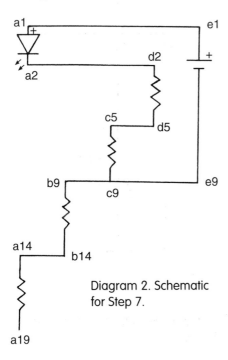

Diagram 2. Schematic for Step 7.

8. Repeat Step 7, but move the negative battery wire into e14 instead of e9 (see Diagram 3).

9. Repeat Step 7, but move the negative battery wire into e19.

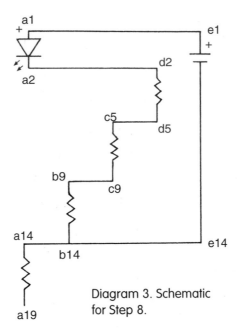

Diagram 3. Schematic for Step 8.

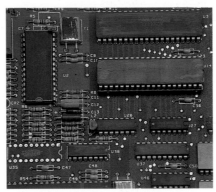

Photo 2. Circuit board from inside a computer, showing colorful resistors, a transistor, capacitors, and many black integrated circuits.

WHAT HAPPENED

In Step 6, with the negative battery wire in e5, the LED shone brightly. When you moved the negative wire from the battery holder from e5 and reconnected it at e9, the LED got duller, because you added another resistor in series to the circuit. Because the resistor was added in series, the current had to flow through each resistor. This increased the resistance in the circuit, which decreased the current, and therefore decreased the amount of light the LED gave off. As you moved the negative wire from e9 to e14, and then from e14 to e19, you added more resistors. When you completed Step 9, you had added a total of 4000 ohms. Resistors are used in many different devices from radios to computers, to adjust the amount of current in electrical systems.

My Circuit Board

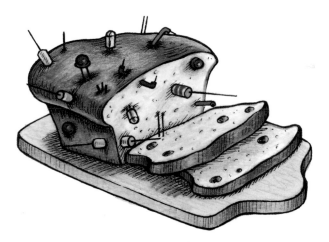

The next few experiments use the same basic circuitry. Rather than putting the identical wiring together each time you do an activity, it is easier to do it once and do it right! This way you will be able to remove the various components and create new connections at the blink of an eye or the flick of a switch. Here is the basic breadboard you will be working from for all the activities in the following pages. Once you construct this basic board, you will not have to take it apart. Only attach the battery when you are doing the actual experiment.

YOU WILL NEED

⇒ small breadboard or socket board (about 300 holes, with lettering and numbering)
⇒ LED (light-emitting diode)
⇒ holder for 2 AA batteries
⇒ 2 AA batteries
⇒ battery connector
⇒ 33-ohm resistor (stripes: red, red, brown, gold)
⇒ 2 pieces of 22 to 24 gauge wire, or pre-bent jump wires*
⇒ wire strippers or cutter (optional)*
⇒ small piece of wood, about the same size as a postcard (optional)

* The function of a jump wire is to connect two parts of the breadboard together. You will need the strippers or cutter if you make your own jump wires.

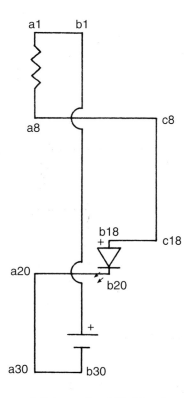

Diagram 1. Schematic of My Circuit Board.

Empty breadboard with jump wires.

WHAT TO DO

1. Push one end of a jump wire into a20 and the other end into a30. If you don't have prebent jump wires, cut them with the wire cutters from the 22- or 24-gauge wire, strip the insulation off the ends, and bend the ends at a right angle. Make them the correct length for the places on the breadboard they need to go to. (See Diagram 1 for Steps 1 to 4.)

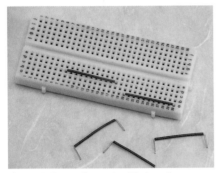

Photo 1. Breadboard with two jump wires.

2. Push one end of a second jump wire into c8 and the other end into c18 (Photo 1).

3. Push the positive terminal (long wire) of an LED into b18, and the negative terminal (short wire) of the LED into b20.

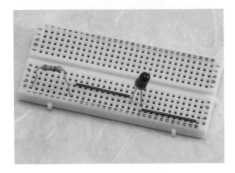

Photo 2. Breadboard with jump wires, LED, and resistors in place.

4. Push one wire end of the resistor into a1 and the other end into a8 (Photo 2).

5. To complete the circuit, place the positive battery lead into b1 and the negative lead into b30. The LED should go on. If the LED doesn't go on, check to see that the positive and negative wires are in the correct holes. Remove one of the battery wires from the board when it is not in use.

6. If you like, you can attach your board to a piece of wood to make it more stable.

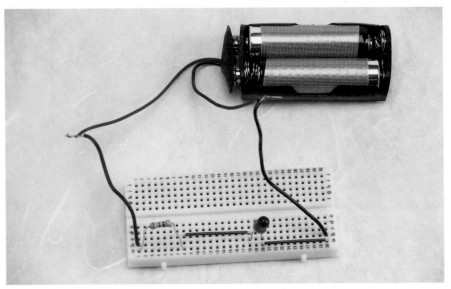

Photo 3. Completed breadboard.

Light Switch

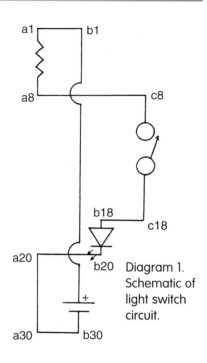

Diagram 1. Schematic of light switch circuit.

When you walk into a dark room, the first thing you do is reach for the light switch. With a flick of your finger, the room is bright—presuming, of course, that the bulbs haven't burned out and the electric bill is paid. How does this happen?

YOU WILL NEED

⇒ My Circuit Board with components (see page 69)
⇒ two-way toggle switch (SPST) with two wires attached

WHAT TO DO

1. Use the basic setup for My Circuit Board, but remove the jump wire from c8 to c18.

2. Place the switch so that the end of one of the wires of the switch is pushed into hole c8 and the end of the other wire is in c18.

3. Turn the switch on and off. What happens to the LED when you do this?

WHAT HAPPENED

When you turned the switch on and off, the LED went on and off. When the switch is off, there is a gap in the circuit and the electrons can't travel through the circuit to light the LED. Turning the switch on closes the gap and the current is restored. When this happens, the LED lights up.

SWITCH ANATOMY

Switches are described by "poles," the number of separate circuits that can be active through a switch at any one time (abbreviated P), and "throws," (abbreviated T), the number of circuit paths that can be controlled by any one pole. The 2-way switch is SPST (single pole, single throw). The three-way switch used on page 72 is SPDT (single pole, double throw).

Flash a Smile

Earlier you made a Leyden jar, a kind of capacitor, something which stored a charge. Let's see how a capacitor affects your circuits.

YOU WILL NEED

⇒ My Circuit Board with components (see page 69)

⇒ 16 V 47 μF (microfarad) capacitor

⇒ 3-way (SPDT) toggle switch

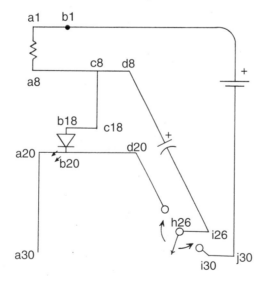

Diagram 1. Schematic of circuit.

WHAT TO DO

1. Use the basic setup for My Circuit Board with the battery wires removed from the board.

2. See Diagram 1 for steps 2 to 5. Push one end wire from a three-way switch into hole d20, push the middle wire into h26, and push the third wire into i30. (Three-way switches have 3 prongs; you may have to attach wires for connection to the circuit board.) The LED remains connected to b18 and b20 as in My Circuit Board.

3. Push the positive wire of the capacitor into d8 and the negative wire into i26.

4. Push the wire attached to the positive terminal of the battery holder into b1 and the negative terminal into j30.

5. When the switch is in the central position, it is off. Move the toggle of the switch from the left "on" position to the right "on" position and back again.

WHAT HAPPENED

When you turned the switch on, connecting i30 with h26, there was a circuit connecting the battery, the resistor, and the capacitor, and the capacitor was

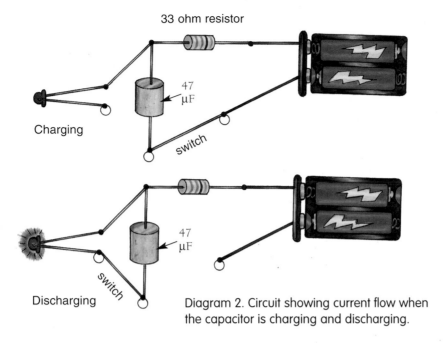

33 ohm resistor

47 μF

Charging

switch

47 μF

Discharging

switch

Diagram 2. Circuit showing current flow when the capacitor is charging and discharging.

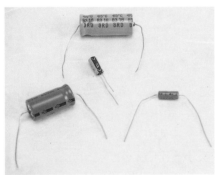

Photo 1. Capacitors.

Photo 3. Camera flash units.

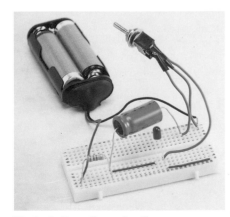

Photo 2. Breadboard with components set up.

charged the charge, which allowed the LED to light (Diagram 2).

A capacitor consists of 2 conductors placed near each other without touching. The space between is filled with an insulator. When the circuit is connected, the battery "pushes" electrons into the capacitor and the electrical charge builds up across the two plates. When the charge is released, the capacitor can provide a very high voltage for a short period of time. Capacitors store electrical energy when they are charged.

The type of circuit we built is called an RC circuit, because it contains a resistor and a capacitor. These circuits are used in devices like cardiac pacemakers, camera flashes and intermittent windshield wipers for cars.

charged, because electrons moved into the capacitor from the circuit. Once there was a charge in the capacitor, it became difficult to charge it further, and the current in the circuit was reduced. When you flipped the switch toggle to the left "on" position, connecting d20 with h26, the circuit from the battery to the capacitor was broken and a new circuit was made connecting the capacitor to the LED. The capacitor dis-

FARADS

The unit of capacitance is the farad (F), named after Michael Faraday (see Human Dynamo). One farad is the capacitance of a capacitor which, charged with one coulomb of charge, has a potential difference of one volt between its plates. One farad is a very large amount of capacitance. Most capacitors produce capacitances in the range of a few millionths of farads (microfarads), abbreviated μF.

Lead the Way

LEAD is a homograph: a word that has two meanings (at least), two pronunciations, and one spelling. In this case you can lead the way using a lead pencil.

YOU WILL NEED

⇒ My Circuit Board with components (see page 69)

⇒ wooden pencil

⇒ craft knife

⇒ two 12-inch (30 cm) pieces of insulated copper wire

⇒ wire strippers

⇒ adult helper

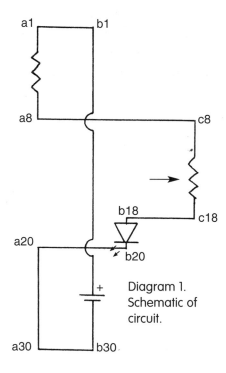

Diagram 1. Schematic of circuit.

WHAT TO DO

1. Have your adult helper remove the wood covering the pencil lead from one side of the pencil using a craft knife.

2. Have an adult use the wire strippers to remove about 1 inch (2.5 cm) of the plastic insulation from both ends of the two pieces of wire.

3. Remove the jump wire that is pushed into c8 and c18 on your circuit board.

4. Place one end of your first piece of copper wire in c8 and let the other end hang over the edge of the electronic board.

5. Place one end of the other copper wire in c18, with the other end hanging over the edge of the electronic board (Photo 1).

6. Touch the free end of one of the copper wires to one end of the pencil lead, and touch the free end of the other copper wire to the other end of the pencil lead. Slide the two bare wires closer together along the pencil lead (Photo 2). Watch what happens to the LED.

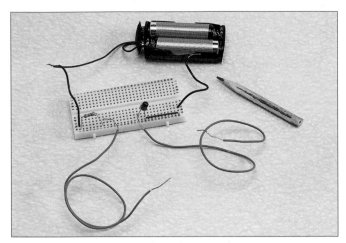

Photo 1. Breadboard setup with wires.

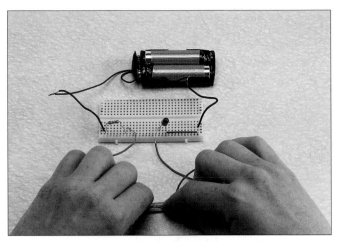

Photo 2. Holding wires close together on pencil lead.

WHAT HAPPENED

When you touched both of the wires to the pencil lead, the LED glowed faintly. As you moved the wires closer together along the pencil lead, the LED became brighter. This is because you have created an adjustable (variable) resistor.

This type of resistor is also called a rheostat or a potentiometer. The pencil lead is made up of a special type of carbon called graphite, which is one of the materials inside commercial resistors.

When you decreased the distance the current had to travel along the pencil lead, you decreased the total amount of resistance in the circuit, and the LED received more current. Rheostats are used to adjust the volume of sound coming from a radio or stereo. They are used in dimmer switches in homes to reduce the brightness of electric lights.

Speed Dial

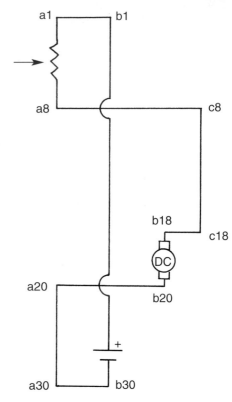

Diagram 1. Schematic of circuit.

Turn on your radio or portable disc player. Adjust the volume. What makes the sound get louder or softer? Here's how to find out.

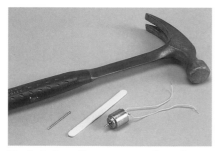

Photo 1. Supplies: motor with craft stick, hammer, and nail.

YOU WILL NEED

⇒ My Circuit Board with components (see page 69)
⇒ small potentiometer
⇒ 2 small pieces of insulated wire
⇒ small nail
⇒ hammer
⇒ craft stick (from ice cream bar)
⇒ 1.5 to 3 V DC electric motor with insulated wires attached

WHAT TO DO

1. Use the setup in My Circuit Board, but remove the resistor and the LED from your circuit board.

2. Attach an insulated wire to the middle post on the potentiometer and attach a second insulated wire to one other potentiometer post. Place the wire connected to the middle post on the potentiometer in hole a1; place the second wire from the potentiometer in a8.

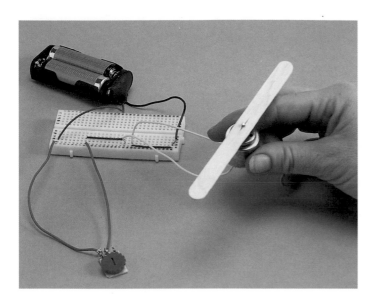

Photo 2. Setup with motor attached.

and watch what happens to the craft stick.

WHAT HAPPENED

You were able to adjust the speed of the motor by turning the potentiometer dial. When you turned the dial on the potentiometer in one direction, the craft stick turned faster. When you turned the dial in the other direction, the stick turned more slowly. A potentiometer varies resistance, as you saw in Lead the Way. Turning the potentiometer moved the connection inside the device to a different position along a coil of resistor material. In one direction, the circuit has only a little resistance; as you turn it in the other direction, the resistance increases.

3. Use a small nail to make a hole in the center of the craft stick just large enough to push the post of the motor through. The craft stick should turn with the motor post.

4. Push the end of one of the wires attached to the motor into b18 and the end of the other motor wire into b20. Hold the motor so that the stick can turn freely.

5.. Insert the wire from the positive battery terminal in b1 and the wire from the negative battery terminal in b30.

6. Turn the potentiometer dial

GLOSSARY

alternating current (AC): An electric current that periodically reverses its direction.

ampere (A): The SI unit of electric current. One ampere is the speed of one coulomb (C) of charge passing a certain point in one second.

atom: The smallest particle of a chemical element that can exist and still have the characteristics of the element.

battery: A number of electrical cells joined together; sometimes used to mean one cell also.

breadboard: A board on which electric circuits may be assembled.

capacitor: A device made of two or more conductors, separated by an insulator, used for storing electric charge.

charge: 1. (n). A property of some particles that causes electrical occurrences. In nature, charges occur as negative or positive. Electric charge is basic to atoms of all substances. The natural unit of electric charge is the charge of an electron, which is negative; it is equal and opposite to the positive charge of a proton. Charge is measured in coulombs (C). 2. The amount of chemical energy stored in a battery that can be changed to electrical energy.

charged (adj.): A condition in which there are more or fewer electrons on an object than there are protons.

circuit: The complete path through which electric current can flow.

conductor: A material that allows electricity to flow through it easily.

conservation of charge: Charges can't be created or destroyed, just moved from one place to another.

coulomb (C): SI unit of electric charge. Equal to the charge transferred by a current of one ampere in one second.

current (I): The movement of electrons along a conductor. Current is measured in amperes.

diode: A gas-filled or semiconductor device with 2 electrodes, which permits flow of current in one direction only.

direct current (DC): An electric current in which the charge flows in one direction.

discharge (n): The release of stored electric charge from a capacitor or battery.

electrochemistry: The field of science that deals with the production of electricity from chemical change or the use of electricity to cause chemical change.

electrode: Conductor that emits or collects electrons in a cell, semiconductor device, etc.

electrolyte: Liquid or paste that conducts electricity as a result of the presence of positive or negative ions.

electromagnet: A temporary magnet produced when a current passes through a coiled wire surrounding an iron core.

electron: Tiny negatively charged particle which is part of all atoms. Each electron carries 0.000 000 000 000 000 000 16 coulombs of charge. Another way to say this is that it takes 6,250,000,000,000,000,000 electrons to carry 1 coulomb of charge.

electrostatic (adj.): Having to do with electric charges at rest, the forces between them, and their electric fields.

farad (F): The standard unit used to measure capacitance. One farad is the amount of capacitance that allows the storage of one coulomb of charge for each volt of the voltage supplied.

fuse: A thin piece of metal of low melting point placed in an electric circuit; designed to melt and break the circuit if a certain amperage is exceeded.

galvanometer: An instrument for detecting and measuring small electric currents.

generator: A machine that changes mechanical energy into electrical energy.

induction: The process by which an electric or magnetic field is produced in a conductor when it is exposed to a changing electric or magnetic field.

insulator: A material that is a poor conductor or nonconductor of electricity.

joule: SI unit of work and energy.

jump wire: A wire used to connect different parts of an electrical circuit.

LED (light-emitting diode): A device that gives off light when an electric current passes through it. Note: the longer leg of the LED is the positive (+) terminal.

Leyden jar: An early capacitor, used to store static charge.

magnet: A piece of metal such as iron which has been magnetized and is surrounded by a magnetic field. It can attract other magnetic metals.

nucleus: The central part of an atom, consisting of neutrons and positively charged protons.

ohm (Ω): Unit of electrical resistance. One ohm is the amount of resistance found between two points on a conductor when a constant potential difference of one volt produces a current of one ampere.

parallel: A way of connecting electrical components so that the current travels through each component separately. Lights connected in parallel will keep shining even if one burns out.

piezoelectric effect: The production of an electric current when certain crystals are subjected to pressure, or the vibration of the crystals caused by an electric current.

potentiometer: Instrument for controlling small potential differences.

repel: To drive or push away.

resistance (R): The property of a conductor to oppose the flow of an electric current. Measured in ohms.

resistor: A device used in an electric circuit to give resistance.

semiconductor: Materials that aren't insulators or conductors, but have electric conductivity between the two. Some examples are boron and silicon.

series: A way of connecting electrical components so that the current travels through each component in turn. All lights connected in series will stop shining if one burns out.

short circuit: An electrical connection between two points that results in a circuit with very low resistance. Usually this is accidental and results in the wires heating up.

SI (Système Internationale): International scientific system of measuring and referring to quantities.

static: 1. (adj.) Standing or fixed in one place. 2. Having to do with motionless electric charges. 3. (n). Atmospheric noise or disturbance resulting from accumulation of electric charges.

switch: A device used to open and close an electric circuit. Switches are described by "poles" (P), the number of separate circuits that can be active through a switch at any one time, and "throws" (T), the number of circuit paths that can be controlled by any one pole. The 2-way switch is SPST (single pole, single throw); the 3-way switch is SPDT (single pole, double throw).

terminal: Point at which a connection is made to an electrical device or system.

transformer: A device that changes the voltage and current of an alternating-current electrical supply by induction.

triboelectric sequence: Listing of materials based on their ability to become positively charged when in contact with other materials.

variable resistor: A resistor that can be adjusted to provide different resistances.

volt (V): The SI unit of potential difference between two points in a circuit. One volt is the potential difference between two points on a conductor carrying a constant current of one ampere when the power used between the points is 1 watt.

watt (W): SI unit of power. One watt of power is the amount in a circuit with a current of one ampere and a voltage of one volt.

INDEX